By **Rachel Bykowski**

STEELE SPRING
STAGE RIGHTS

www.stagerights.com

For all stage performance inquiries, please contact:

Steele Spring Stage Rights
3845 Cazador Street
Los Angeles, CA 90065
(323) 739-0413
www.stagerights.com

CAST OF CHARACTERS

Cast Total: 3F

CAMARO GIBSON: Female, late 30s, any race or ethnicity. Camaro loves three things in this life: strawberry glazed donuts from Dunkin' Donuts, her daddy, and his 1967 Chevy Camaro. She got an engine for a heart and oil for blood. Don't try to change her. Stubborn as all hell, just like her daddy.

ASTON GIBSON: Female, mid-30s, any race or ethnicity. Camaro's cousin on government papers, but to the family (where it counts) they are sisters. Aston is a night shift RN and taking classes to become a nurse practitioner. Used to be a wild child when she was younger, still is at heart. She got a mouth and a temper that goes from 0 to 60 in three seconds flat.

LUCY "LUCKY" WELLS: Female, late 20s, any race or ethnicity. Sergeant in the U.S. Marine Corps. Confident 'cause she knows her shit, but still "lost" in the way every twenty-something is lost. You give her an inch, she'll take hundred miles 'cause she is just that good.

DIALECTS

Yes, the characters are from Chicago.
No, they should not sound like SNL's "Super Fans."

CASTING

Inclusive casting is <u>required</u>. The play's casting <u>must</u> reflect the diversity of the Southwest Side of Chicago.

TIME

Now: from October-June.

PLACE

The garage of Gibson & Sons' Automotive Repair Shop.
Southwest Side of Chicago: the West Lawn neighborhood.

SET DESCRIPTION

Inside of the car garage of Gibson & Sons' Automotive Repair Shop. The garage is the definition of organized clutter. Things are rusted and every surface is covered in dirt or oil. In the middle of the garage is an old 1967 convertible Chevy Camaro. The engine is displayed prominently in the front. The body is rusted away and is missing all the essential parts of its body. Throughout the play, the Chevy becomes more and more completed with windows, windshield, doors, mirrors, tires, steering wheel, etc.

NOTES

// indicates the line is interrupted by the following line of dialogue.

RUN TIME

105 minutes

AUTHOR'S NOTES

Rev celebrates the tradition of the fighting middle class wanting more for its future generations. The play demonstrates the fortitude, strength, and vulnerability of the American woman. The dream all Americans have for future generations to do better than the last. This play will explore how women contribute to the legacies of their families, break tradition, and help carve the landscape of America's hometowns and their own family histories.

Rev is a love letter to my childhood home on the Southwest Side of Chicago: West Lawn. This play is dedicated to all the people and places that shaped me into the woman I am today. This play is for my mother, father, and brother. It is for my best friend who lived three houses down from me while we were experiencing our own "Emily-like" moments in life. It is for 64th Street and ambling down Lawndale in my blue and gold uniform on my way to St. Nicholas of Tolentine Elementary School. The play is full of memories, like riding the #54 CTA bus up and down Pulaski and the first time I rode the orange line by myself, looked out the window after the train passed Halsted, and watched the Chicago skyline come into view.

West Lawn is a residential neighborhood that is full of generations of families. It is a community of middle, working-class people that help each other when their paychecks can't quite cut it. We shovel each other's walkways. We pass delicious barbeque across fences. We work out of garages fixing everything we own by hand and trade goods with each other in our alleys to help our neighbors get the job done.

West Lawn is home to numerous cultures and ethnicities. Businesses like Gibson & Sons' Automotive Repair Shop must reflect the West Lawn community. It is required that any production of *Rev* must showcase the diversity of West Lawn and show respect and gratitude for each character's hard work and sacrifice.

Despite the play's opening description of a car garage full of car parts, work tables, and clutter, I always keep a black box theatre in mind. The garage, along with the Chevy Camaro, can be as grand or as minimal as the theatre's space and budget allows. Let your designers step-up to the challenge and trust in your audiences' imaginations.

REV

AUTHOR'S NOTES (CONT'D)

There are moments of silence, beats, and pauses throughout the play. Those are not suggestions. The pace of the dialogue is brisk. Each character has work to get done and places to be; none of them have time to sugar coat or dally. Especially in the scenes between Camaro and Aston, who can already predict the next words out of each other's mouth. When a silence, a pause, or beat hits, the audience should feel it too. Sometimes the silence will feel like a breath of fresh air as we travel down a memory. Other times, it will feel like a punch in the gut.

The core of my mission as a playwright is to explore the many facets of womanhood. In many instances, to be a woman means pain, silence, humiliation, and loneliness. However, being a woman can also mean strength, endurance, vulnerability, and love. I feel that often women writers are influenced or pressured into believing that their stories only matter when their characters endure some kind of extreme trauma. That trauma is usually translated into a rape, assault, harassment, or putting her literal life on the line. I wrote *Rev* to prove that is not true. I do not need to inflict violence on a woman's body to assert the importance of her life and goal.

There is value in stories about women living paycheck to paycheck, women trying to raise a family, women going for a promotion, women and female friendships, women falling in and out of love, women fucking up and learning (or not) from their mistakes, and women finding themselves in the pages of their family history. There is value in a woman's smile (not just her tears) as she looks at her accomplishments, flaws, and this thing she calls life.

SCENE 1

Lights up on the inside of the car garage of Gibson & Sons' Automotive Repair Shop in early October. The large, hand-carved wooden sign boasting "Gibson & Sons" prominently hangs on the center wall of the garage. The garage is the perfect definition of organized clutter. Every section of the garage boasts some kind of tool or car part. Things are rusted and every surface is covered in dirt or oil, but there are love, hard work, and memories in each of those stains. Far upstage right is a door that leads to the outside. Next to that door are a mini fridge and a coat rack with an extra jumpsuit hanging on it. Further downstage is a metal worktable. Far downstage left is a swinging door that leads offstage where the shop's small customer lobby and second garage are located. Upstage left of the swinging door is a tall, chest-high counter with a landline phone and the door to the office. In the middle of the garage is an old 1967 convertible Chevy Camaro, although you wouldn't know that just by looking at it. It's missing all four tires, lights, mirrors, both of its doors, the steering wheel, and the hood. Its engine is displayed prominently in the front. What remains of the car's body is an oxidized, blood brown color, but you can feel this car lived its best life once upon a time. CAMARO is working diligently under the car. All we can see are her feet sticking out of the side. We hear her clanging away, mumbling and cursing a little under her breath. ASTON enters from the upstage right door carrying two coffees and a brown bag from Dunkin' Donuts. She is wearing her nursing scrubs and her hair is in a messy bun. She is tired from working the night shift, but it's her frustration and the coffee that are giving her adrenaline.

ASTON: I swear to God, Camaro! I swear to God, Jesus, Mary, Joseph, all the angels and saints, I'll even turn to the devil if he'll listen to me! That girl... that girl is gonna... I'm gonna leave. // That's it, I'm gone.

CAMARO *(still working under the car)*: Take it // easy, Aston.

ASTON: I got the money! You know I do. Got the money. Been saving for five years. Take it all and // just disappear.

> *CAMARO continues to work under the car throughout ASTON's rant. She's heard this all before.*

CAMARO: Ya ain't goin' nowhere // and ya know it.

ASTON: Then, oh my Lord, Steve is NO help. He calls me while I'm on my shift so, obviously, I can't answer // my phone.

CAMARO: Obviously.

ASTON: It's 2:30 in the God blessed morning. I'm in the middle of my rounds, trying to finish up so I can grab one bite of my baby carrots before someone goes into cardiac arrest. 'Cause you know something, Camaro? You wanna know // something?

CAMARO: Ya gotta // feelin'.

ASTON: I gotta feeling! I got a God blessed feeling that at 3 o'clock on the dot someone, someone in that hospital was gonna have a grabber. And wouldn't you know it... // BAM!

CAMARO: Bam.

ASTON: Mr. Helminski in C4 decides he wants to try to meet his maker. But you wanna // know something?

CAMARO: Ya were right by // his room.

ASTON: God gave me that feeling for a reason and put me right next to Mr. Helminski's room. Something told me // to check on him.

CAMARO: That feelin'.

ASTON: So, meanwhile, I'm trying to perform a miracle and I can feel my phone vibrating and vibrating // over and over again.

CAMARO: Steve won't let // up.

ASTON: I got that feeling again. Feeling ON TOP OF feeling // I knew it was 'bout Emily.

CAMARO: You knew it was 'bout Emily.

ASTON: I swear to God! That man can't do anything when it comes to that girl! He can run straight into a burning building, but when it comes to Emily he turns // into mush.

CAMARO: Into mush.

ASTON: So, it's now 6 a.m. and I'm an hour away from being done with this shift and I look down at my phone and see ten, TEN missed calls and 'bout one hundred different texts from Steve // all 'bout Emily.

CAMARO finally pushes herself out from under the car.

CAMARO: Is it the same boy? He gotta weird name, right?

ASTON: Blaise...

CAMARO: Ooohhh, you're in trouble.

ASTON: Emily was supposed to be spending the night at Kristen's house. BUT Kristen's dad stops by the fire station and guess what he said...

CAMARO: Emily // wasn't there.

ASTON: Emily hasn't been there all day!

CAMARO: I can't believe ya fell for that. You used to pull that shit all the time with your li'l high school boyfriends. Drove Daddy crazy.

ASTON: I raised her better.

CAMARO: She's your daughter, Aston.

ASTON: Kristen spilled the beans real quick after her mom threatened to take away Homecoming.

CAMARO: Where's Blaise's parents?

ASTON: Out of town 'til the weekend. Vacation in the middle of the week!

CAMARO: Well, ya know, they live in New Lenox.

ASTON: I don't wanna go home and deal with her.

CAMARO: Well, at least not 'til I had my breakfast.

> *ASTON reaches into the Dunkin' Donuts bag and hands CAMARO a veggie flatbread sandwich. Camaro is confused and stares at the food.*

ASTON: Veggie egg white on flatbread. I got one too. It's better for you, Camaro.

CAMARO: I ain't interested in your new diet for the week.

ASTON: Seventeen days going strong and look...

> *She stretches out her pants.*

...they're loose.

CAMARO: Only took ya seventeen years to lose that baby weight.

ASTON: Shut up.

CAMARO: I like the way I am.

> *CAMARO tosses the flatbread in the trashcan and holds out her hand. ASTON reaches into the bag and pulls out a strawberry glazed donut. Camaro takes a huge bite.*

ASTON: At least wash your hands first.

CAMARO: Oil makes the strawberry glaze taste better. Gets into my system. I become one with the car.

> *They both lean against the counter and eat in silence. They have the same mannerisms when chewing.*

ASTON: Is today the day?

CAMARO: Could be. Gotta finish breakfast, then I'll see if he wants to rev.

> *They sit back in silence again and continue to chew.*

Emily on birth control?

ASTON: No. One of her little friends told her that birth control makes you gain weight so she won't even touch the stuff. I told her, I said, you wanna know what makes you gain weight?

CAMARO & ASTON: A baby.

CAMARO: What are you gonna do 'bout her?

ASTON: Lord if I know. I'm supposed to take her to get her nails done for Homecoming today, but I can't even stand to look at her.

CAMARO: Then don't // do it.

ASTON: I had to threaten Steve to go pick her up from that boy's house, but he didn't wanna go. He said, "Can't you do it on your way home from your shift?"

CAMARO: Mush.

ASTON: He hasn't even been a year on the job, but that man has already stared down flames that are 20 feet high, but he melts in front of a five-foot girl he helped create.

CAMARO: Daddy was the same way... with you at least.

ASTON: He was rough with both of us.

CAMARO: Didn't know no better.

ASTON: Doesn't make it right.

CAMARO: It made us strong. You gotta make Emily strong.

ASTON: I will NEVER lay a hand on her.

CAMARO: Don't be so dramatic. The man didn't abuse us. There's a big difference between people who beat their kids and what Daddy did: one quick slap across the face when we were mouthin' off. In fact, I bet you can count on one hand and not use all your fingers, the amount of times he slapped you. But you were Daddy's girl through and through. His princess. He put you up on that pedestal and admit it, you loved the view.

ASTON: It came with some perks.

CAMARO: You were nuthin' but a wild child. You deserved all ten fingers AND toes.

ASTON: You got all ten fingers.

CAMARO: I'm the oldest. The guinea pig.

ASTON: You didn't deserve it.

CAMARO: It set me straight, didn't it? Whatever I did, I made damn sure not to do again. Maybe you should try with Emily. One quick slap and I guarantee she won't dare try another sleepover—

ASTON: —No, I gotta do better by her.

CAMARO: Then take her off the pedestal and start with her nails.

ASTON: Yeah, yeah. I guess you're right.

CAMARO: Don't be mush.

ASTON: I won't.

> They sit back in silence. CAMARO finishes her donut.

Oh, here. I got you another.

> ASTON pulls out a second strawberry glazed donut.

CAMARO: Egg whites and two donuts? Whaddya want?

ASTON: I can't treat my big sister?

> *CAMARO stares at the donut. She is skeptical.*

I felt like today might be THE day and we would need something to celebrate.

> *CAMARO cautiously takes the donut and bites into it.*

Ready?

CAMARO: Let's do it.

> *ASTON goes to the passenger side of the Chevy and loudly clears her throat. CAMARO smiles and pretends to open the nonexistent door for her. This is part of their ritual.*

You're such a daddy's girl.

> *CAMARO runs to the other side of the car and waits for ASTON to reach over and mime unlocking the other nonexistent door. Camaro hops in and excitedly pretends to grip the nonexistent steering wheel.*

ASTON: Whcrc we going?

CAMARO: To the beginnin' of the end.

ASTON: The end AND the beginning.

CAMARO: Route 66.

ASTON: Oh! Can we take Lake Shore up? I love that drive.

CAMARO: It's 8:30 in the mornin'. We'll be in the heat of rush hour.

ASTON: I don't care! Anywhere you stop, you just look out the window and... there it is.

CAMARO: Water to the east. Skyscrapers to the west.

ASTON: It's October so the lake will be that pretty aqua green I love. And the lights... I never need to see stars if I can see those gorgeous, manmade constellations.

CAMARO: Once again... 8:30 in the mornin', so the lights won't be on.

ASTON: Fine! Drop me off by the Field Museum. I'll take my time walking through the campus and by the time the sun sets, I'll be on my way to the Mag Mile for some shopping.

CAMARO: Nordstrom's Rack.

ASTON: Shut up! Try Neimans, then Burberry, then Weitzman, then I'll check myself into one of those hotels I got no business being in and eat food that is more expensive than me.

CAMARO: You got that much cash saved?

ASTON: Ahem... one-thousand ten dollars.

CAMARO: Alright, alright. If ya want, I can drop ya off. It's right on my way.

ASTON: The beginning.

CAMARO: And the end.

ASTON: Route 66.

CAMARO: Start at Adams and Michigan, south to Springfield, then St. Louis, cut through Oklahoma, Texas, New Mexico, Arizona, and in ten days, there ya are...

ASTON: Water to the west, buildings to the east.

CAMARO: California.

> *CAMARO closes her eyes and takes a deep breath.*

ASTON: So... what are you waiting for?

CAMARO: I've never seen the ocean.

ASTON: And...?

CAMARO: I'm tryin' smell it.

> *ASTON reaches into the glove compartment and pulls out a set of keys.*

Okay...

> *They close their eyes.*

ASTON: What's on the radio?

CAMARO: Oh! Daddy's favorite song! The one where he'd make us dance on his feet.

ASTON: "My Girl."

> *Complete silence. CAMARO and ASTON sway to the tune of "My Girl" playing in their heads. Camaro places the key in the ignition. She stops and looks at Aston.*

CAMARO: For Daddy...

ASTON: Ugh... alright.

ASTON & CAMARO: Old Style sittin' in the console

Wind blowin' through the window

When the rubber meets the concrete

Ya get down on your knees

Pray for your shot

Grab life by the balls and give it all ya got.

> *They spit.*

CAMARO: Let's see if he'll rev.

CAMARO closes her eyes and turns the key. The engine immediately coughs, stalls, then makes a clunking sound that ends with a loud pop. CAMARO and ASTON, defeated, get out of the car. CAMARO tends to the engine.

CAMARO (CONT'D): Well... fuck.

ASTON: Well, it's not like you could go right away. I mean, you still need some doors, a hood, tires, paint, steering wheel—

CAMARO: —Gotta start with the heart first.

ASTON: Maybe the engine is busted.

CAMARO: It's Daddy's heart.

ASTON: Isn't that what killed him?

CAMARO: I'll make him rev again.

ASTON: It's from the 60s.

CAMARO: You can't kill a 1967 Chevy Camaro. He's too strong, too fast, too—

ASTON: —Stubborn.

CAMARO: He'll rev again.

ASTON: Fine, fine, I know I won't get anywhere with you. You're too much like Daddy.

CAMARO: Thank you.

ASTON: Lot looks full.

CAMARO: That's right.

ASTON: Gonna be a busy day... maybe.

CAMARO: You don't gotta admit you were wrong.

ASTON: Not wrong yet.

CAMARO: Look at that lot. Things are pickin' back up.

ASTON: Nothing to worry 'bout.

CAMARO: That's right.

ASTON: Just a slump.

CAMARO: Just a big ol' dip.

ASTON: Hell of a hole for three years.

CAMARO: And I'm busy fillin' it.

ASTON: You're filling it with something.

CAMARO: People like the car. It reminds them of Daddy. It's like an attraction.

ASTON: Or a distraction.

CAMARO: I don't tell you how to draw blood, do I?

ASTON: This is my shop too.

CAMARO: Daddy left it to me. I got the papers.

ASTON: Which papers you talking 'bout? 'Cause I got some too.

CAMARO: You got somethin' to say, little sister?

ASTON: I just want to help.

CAMARO: You already helped enough.

ASTON: When I look out that door, I see a lot finally full of potential again and we got two garages here, but only one of them you can do real work in. People like us. They like our family. They liked Daddy. But Daddy isn't here anymore. He's been gone five years and people aren't gonna wait on their cars to get fixed 'cause you're busy tinkering with the past.

CAMARO: I just want to hear it rev again, Aston. One last time. Lemme hear the heartbeat, then I'll let it go.

ASTON: I'll believe it when I see it.

CAMARO: When have I ever lied to you?

ASTON: This is your shop now. I want you to start acting like it. Make decisions.

CAMARO: I'm makin' lots of decisions

ASTON: Shake things up bit. Like this... the sign. The sign says, "Gibson & Sons."

CAMARO: Daddy was hopeful.

ASTON: Daddy was wrong. You should start there and make it your own.

CAMARO: If it ain't broke, don't fix it.

ASTON: Then, I dunno, maybe try hiring more people. You know we got plenty of cousins.

CAMARO: Nick and Marty will be comin' in soon. We'll plow through that lot with one garage tied behind our backs.

ASTON: Nick will probably call off again and Marty will be passing out in the lobby by noon. But, you know, Emily gets out of school at 2:00...

CAMARO: I knew I shouldn't of eaten that donut.

ASTON: She can be here by 2:30.

CAMARO: No.

ASTON: She can help in the office. Sort through the papers, answer phones—

CAMARO: —Hell no.

ASTON: She's your niece.

CAMARO: And that's why I'm sayin' FUCK no. The only thing that girl knows how to do is take selfies and post on Instagram. She's just lucky she's pretty.

ASTON: How can you say that?

CAMARO: 'Cause she's my niece.

ASTON: Emily needs direction. You know, structure. Something that will keep her motivated that isn't how many likes she gets on Instagram.

CAMARO: You want me to be a babysitter.

ASTON: I want her to take pride in herself and hard work. I dunno, I think it'll show her she's more than just a pretty selfie.

CAMARO: She should play to her strengths and that ain't what's in her head.

ASTON: Will you quit being a jerk and just... Look, I know this might be difficult for you to understand 'cause you don't have kids—

CAMARO: —Here we go! How's that my // problem?

ASTON: This is just a blind spot for you. When you have a child, you are literally their ENTIRE world. Daddy was like a god to us and everything he touched: our house, our school, this garage, everything was a part of that world. We didn't need anything beyond that. Emily's world is our house, Archer Avenue, her high school, Kristen, Blaise, New Lenox. Do you know what she told me? Blaise's parents finished their basement and she could move down there with him if she still didn't figure out what college she wants to go to yet.

CAMARO: Nuthin' wrong New Lenox—

ASTON: —Camaro—

CAMARO: —She has time, Aston.

ASTON: I want her dreams to be bigger than a New Lenox finished basement. I'm waiting, waiting for the day she realizes she is smarter than me. I don't want her to be AS smart as me.

CAMARO: Aston, if Emily turns out even half as smart as you, no basement nowhere on the Southside will keep her. She's just bein' seventeen.

ASTON: Right, and I was just being seventeen in Steve's parent's basement...

CAMARO: Ya turned out alright. Took some extra time to get there—

ASTON: —Seventeen years—

CAMARO: —But now look at ya. High school graduate—

ASTON: —G.E.D.—

CAMARO: —RN and soon to be doctor—

ASTON: —Nurse. Practitioner.

CAMARO: Emily's got some big shoes to fill.

ASTON: I'm scared, Camaro. I'm scared of that boy.

CAMARO: Why? Did somethin'— Did he do somethin' to // Emily?!

ASTON: Are you crazy? I'd be asking you to help bury a body right now.

CAMARO: You don't get scared.

ASTON: Have you seen her recently?

CAMARO: 'Bout a month ago. She's my curly Sue again.

ASTON: Was... this week, she's back to stick straight.

CAMARO: How many times did ya change your hair?

ASTON: I never changed it for a boy.

CAMARO: She did this before. First week of high school.

ASTON: That was awful. Her gorgeous curls just fried straight. But I get that. Fourteen, new school, new neighborhood, no friends...girls are vicious. That was survival, but this...this is different.

CAMARO: She wants to be liked.

ASTON: If I would of known sending her off to some private school would introduce her to that boy—

CAMARO: —Kennedy was good enough for us. Hell, Emily could of rolled outta bed into class.

ASTON: They didn't have a drama program.

CAMARO: How many plays she been in since?

ASTON: You know teenagers.

CAMARO: That's exactly what I'm sayin'! So, she straightens her hair a bit? Okay, all the girls from that neighborhood do. She did what she had to do to get a seat at the lunch table. Now, she got friends down there and she let 'er curl back in—

ASTON: —Then she met Blaise. He told her that he thought she looked "so hot" with straight hair. I just—

CAMARO: —You did the right thing. She wanted to be in the drama club, Kennedy didn't have one. Ya wanted her to learn 'bout Jesus and the walkin' dead, Kennedy was public—

ASTON: —I didn't want her trekking Archer Avenue on the same path as me. God knew I was being selfish and my punishment is no sleep. Just nightmares 'bout finished basements in New Lenox.

CAMARO: I love Emily. She's my blood. But I ain't lookin' to be no one's mom. You think I'm like Daddy. But sometimes when I look in the mirror, I see her. My nightmare.

ASTON: I really wish you'd stop talking 'bout your mom // like that.

CAMARO: Aston, you lemme talk 'bout my mother any way I want.

ASTON: I just believe-

CAMARO: —She's a swerver. A left instead of a right...

ASTON: Fine.

CAMARO: I mean, fuck, what mother is so checked-out of her family, she lets her husband name their daughter after a car.

ASTON: I dunno. Ever since I had Emily... I'm starting to understand her now, that's all.

CAMARO: Don't say that.

ASTON: Blind spot for you.

CAMARO: When it comes to that woman, it's a permanent blind spot by choice.

ASTON: You need help around here. Just an extra hand. The less time you spend in the office, the faster you can finish the cars in the lot, and the more time you can spend trying to get this rusted thing to start.

CAMARO: I'm so close now.

ASTON: You've been saying that for five years. Either this antique is gonna start or you're just... stalling.

CAMARO: And why the fuck would I do that? You don't think I wanna clear this outta here and make room for more cash to flow in? I mean, damn, I forgot what this place looks like without the Chevy in it.

ASTON: Spacious.

CAMARO: Empty.

> Beat.

ASTON: Camaro, I can't do it again. You know, I finally started those night classes and with Emily getting ready to go off to college—

CAMARO: —Am I askin' you for anythin'?

ASTON: No, you never do. But this letter does...

> ASTON takes a letter out of her purse and hands It to CAMARO.

CAMARO: Where did you get this?

ASTON: I got a key to that office, same as you.

CAMARO: Snoopin'.

ASTON: It's not snooping in your own home. You promised me, three years ago, that you wouldn't let this slip again. When I wrote you that check, you said that was the last time I would ever see the word "foreclosure" in big red letters.

CAMARO: It's just a piece of paper. A reminder of a final // notice of payment.

ASTON: I couldn't even go to ONE night class. I could barely look the admissions person in the face as I begged for my tuition back.

CAMARO: You made that decision. I never asked you for a penny.

ASTON: I don't wanna see my home close.

CAMARO: I got it under control, ya hear me? I'm the big sister. I'll take care of us.

ASTON: Prove it.

CAMARO: Aston... this is not just metal and oil. It was left to rust and die. I gotta remind it of its purpose for livin'. That takes a lot more work than just tightenin' a few screws. I'm tryin' to make a heart beat again.

ASTON: You get it to rev and then you let it go.

CAMARO: I swear on Daddy's heart. Once I hear that heartbeat, I will let it go.

A bell rings. A customer is waiting.

CAMARO: Bet that's the Old Cunt.

ASTON: Mrs. Wilson just needs to get rid of that old junker already.

CAMARO: She don't like to be kept waitin'. She's got a lot of cats to get home to and feed.

ASTON: I better get home and deal with my mess. Steve has probably locked himself in the bathroom, so he doesn't have deal with Emily.

CAMARO: The longest shit in the world.

ASTON: Gotta coax him out, take Emily to school, get me to class, then get her nails done.

CAMARO: I thought you said—

ASTON: —It's Blaise's Homecoming tomorrow. I can't have her go to New Lenox with Archer and Normandy Avenue looking nails. You'd understand if—

CAMARO: —Blind spot. Got it. Her nails more important than your sleep?

ASTON: We're just going over ethics and polices today. I'll sum it up for you, "Keep your patient alive."

CAMARO: Well, thanks for that lesson, Dr. Gibson.

ASTON: Ha... right, if Emily doesn't kill me first.

CAMARO: You'll be runnin' your own practice before ya know it.

ASTON: Let's hope it doesn't take another seventeen years. See you next week.

CAMARO: I gotta feelin'.

ASTON: Might be the day.

CAMARO: The beginnin' of the end.

ASTON: The end AND the beginning.

ASTON exits. Lights fade.

End Scene 1.

SCENE 2

Lights up on the garage a little later that morning. CAMARO is talking on the garage's landline phone.

CAMARO: Yes, Mrs. Wilson I understand... I understand, I know, Fridays are very important 'cause that's when ya go grocery shoppin'... Normally, that wouldn't be a problem, but ya need more than an oil change. Your check engine light was on and...

The bell rings. A customer is waiting.

Yes, Mrs. Wilson, I'm doin' what my dad would do. We fix cars in the order we getum... Uh huh... Yes... Yes... But ya see, the reason ya car won't start ain't 'cause of the oil... Well, it's probably a busted or missin' piston ring, trust me, I know these things. It's a thin, metal ring, but it'll do the trick... uh huh... Oh my God! You have to take who to the hospital...?! Oh, your cat. Is that a new one...? It is. Lucky number seven huh...?

LUCY "LUCKY" enters from the swinging door. CAMARO notices her and is a bit confused. LUCKY mouths something along the lines of, "Hello." Camaro looks frustrated and mouths back, "Where's Marty?" Lucky mouths back, "What?" Camaro covers the phone.

(In a loud, hushed tone)

Marty?

LUCKY looks around and shrugs.

(Back to phone)

Uh huh... Oh, that's nice... He sounds like a sweet cat...

CAMARO stretches the phone cord as long as it'll go and walks out the swinging door. She nearly wraps LUCKY in the cord.

Ya know, Mrs. Wilson, I'm not really a cat person, but I guess their um, poop, isn't supposed to be green... uh huh...

CAMARO reenters, still on the phone, and runs LUCKY over with the cord. She shoos LUCKY over to the corner.

And it's all over your house too? I'm sure Mr. Wilson didn't like that... I understand, but Mrs. Wilson, at least three other cars came in before ya so, I gotta take care of them as well. I can have your car ready by 2... Mrs. Wilson! Please, please calm down! You don't gotta go grocery shoppin' right at noon...! I'm sorry... I'm sorry I didn't mean to get snippy... No, my dad would not appreciate that tone either... Oka-okay! Mrs. Wilson, I'll do my best, how 'bout that... Okay, okay! I'll try to see ya at noon, but Mrs. Wilson—

Mrs. Wilson hangs up.

CAMARO (CONT'D) *(to herself)*: Fuckin' Old Cunt...

LUCKY: She sounds like my grandma.

CAMARO: Can I help you?

LUCKY: Didn't mean to bug ya, but the guy in your lobby is passed out.

CAMARO: Yeah... I guess Marty decided to take his mid-mornin' nap a li'l earlier than usual.

LUCKY: I think he's drunk.

CAMARO: Are ya droppin' off a car?

LUCKY: No, no. I don't got one. I just noticed your lot is pretty full.

CAMARO: Yeah, and water is wet.

LUCKY: I'm Lucky.

CAMARO: I'm... not?

LUCKY: My name... It's Lucy, but everyone calls me Lucky.

CAMARO: Are ya sellin' somethin'? Ya gotta kid in the Girl Scouts or some shit?

LUCKY: No, I don't—

CAMARO: —Look, I'll buy a box of Thin Mints from ya, but right now, if ya don't got a car for me // to fix—

LUCKY notices the Chevy Camaro.

LUCKY: Camaro...

CAMARO: What?

LUCKY: The car... this is a 1967 Chevy Camaro, right? Who ya buildin' this for?

CAMARO: You know cars?

LUCKY: Sergeant Wells, MOS 3521.

CAMARO: [...]

LUCKY: I was... am a Marine, 8 years.

CAMARO *(not impressed)*: Oo fuckin' rah. Thanks for your service.

LUCKY: I worked motor T and was pretty damn good at it.

CAMARO: Look, Sergeant, I'm sure our nation thanks ya, but I got four cars I gotta finish by noon or I'm gonna have a couple of unhappy costumers includin' one old lady with a sick cat.

LUCKY: I can help. I brought a resume in case ya wanted to see it. A lot is just my military background. I've worked on tanks, HMMWVs, things like that—

LUCKY hands her resume to CAMARO.

CAMARO: Look, Lucy...

LUCKY: Lucky.

CAMARO: I ain't hirin'.

LUCKY: You're at least fifteen cars deep in your lot.

CAMARO: We'll get to them.

LUCKY: Your only other mechanic is "napping" at 10:30 in the mornin'.

CAMARO: Marty works better in the afternoons. Besides, he's not my ONLY other mechanic. He'll be comin' in anytime now—

> *The phone starts ringing. CAMARO answers.*

Gibson & Sons'... Nick, you're runnin' late... Are you fuckin' serious...? No, no, you listen! We are...

> *Notices LUCKY is listening. CAMARO stretches the phone out the swinging door. We can still hear her.*

We are fuckin' fifteen cars deep, Marty is drunk, passed out in the lobby, and I got four cars to finish by noon... I dunno, her fuckin' cat is dyin' or some shit... Nick! Aunt Rita's pies ain't gonna save you... no, I don't need to talk to your mom—

> *Her tone changes to sweetness.*

Hi, Aunt Rita... Oh, I'll bet Nick's very sick... Oh, ya know, cold season is comin' around... No, I'm fine. Haven't caught it yet...

> *CAMARO reenters still on the phone.*

Yes, yes... I'll be sure to stay bundled up. Someone's gotta be healthy enough to work, right? MMhmmm... Okay, okay, ya really don't gotta... Apple pie is fine... Yes, okay... Hope Nick feels better. Love ya...

> *CAMARO hangs up the phone. She goes over the mini fridge and pulls out an Old Style beer. She walks back to the Chevy Camaro and hops in. She cracks open the beer, takes a long swig, and stares straight ahead.*

> *Silence.*

LUCKY: Was that your other, OTHER ONLY mechanic?

CAMARO: Two cars by noon.

LUCKY: What?

CAMARO: You deaf, Sergeant? I said, two cars by noon. Think ya can handle it?

> *LUCKY walks over to the mini fridge and pulls out a beer*

LUCKY: I'll do ya one better... I'll finish all four.

> *LUCKY cracks open the beer, but CAMARO grabs the beer out of her hand before she can drink.*

CAMARO: Beer's for employees only.

LUCKY: All four by noon.

CAMARO: Includin' Mrs. Wilson's?

LUCKY: I'll make that Old Cunt purr.

>*CAMARO chugs one of the beers (maybe both).*

CAMARO: Ooh fuckin' rah.

>*Lights fade.*
>
>*End of Scene 2.*

SCENE 3

Lights up on the garage with CAMARO under the 1967 Chevy. It is Monday of the following week. ASTON enters from the outside door carrying a Dunkin' Donuts bag. Camaro is working under the Chevy.

ASTON: That's it! That is it! I'm done, Camaro. You hear me? I'm packing my bags and // I'm leaving.

CAMARO: Ya only got one thousand dollars // saved up.

ASTON: One thousand and ten.

CAMARO: Ya ain't goin' nowhere.

ASTON: You watch me. One-thousand ten dollars? I can stay in one of those nice rooms at the Peninsula downtown for a // weekend.

CAMARO: What would ya // do there?

ASTON: You know what they got above each of their beds in that hotel? Doorbells. Yeah... And what you do is, you get into your pajamas, wash your face, brush your teeth, you know, get yourself all ready for bed, and you ring that doorbell and someone will come up and tuck. You. In.

CAMARO pushes herself out from under the car.

CAMARO: What?

ASTON: Swear to God.

CAMARO: Why would a grown ass person—

ASTON: —Because why the fuck not.

CAMARO: Ooookkkay, what did Emily do now?

ASTON: Oh no, it's not JUST Emily.

CAMARO: Steve?

ASTON: Steve has probably barricaded himself in the bathroom. He just got hooked on Breaking Bad so, he might live in there now.

CAMARO: So, Blaise?

ASTON: Worse. Bebe...

CAMARO: Bebe?

ASTON: Blaise's mother.

CAMARO: Bebe...?

ASTON: Bebe Bennington.

CAMARO: Wait a second... so, Blaise Bennington.

ASTON: B.B.

CAMARO: Like his mom?

ASTON: She LOVES her boy.

CAMARO: Oooooohhhhhh, you're in trouble.

ASTON: Saturday was the New Lenox Homecoming—

CAMARO: —You took Emily to get her nails // done.

ASTON: Don't start with me // on that.

CAMARO: I'm just sayin'...

ASTON: I gave her a curfew.

CAMARO: Really? On Homecomin'?

ASTON: Dance ends at 10. She needed to be home by midnight.

CAMARO: Seems fair.

ASTON: Cinderella got home by midnight and so can she.

CAMARO: No one else had a curfew though.

ASTON: 12:01 rolls around. I am five hours deep into my shift and I get // that feeling...

CAMARO: That feelin'.

ASTON: I call the house phone. No one answers. I call Steve at the firehouse. Some building burning down on the Southwest Side. He runs to those flames. No fear in his eyes, but when I tell him it's 12:03 and no one is picking up the house phone, he tells me to calm down.

CAMARO: Mush.

ASTON: Mush.

CAMARO: You call Emily.

ASTON: No. I know this game.

CAMARO: You got that feelin'.

ASTON: I got that feeling! An angel whispering in my ear, "Call Bebe."

CAMARO: You didn't.

ASTON: I did. Bebe answers. There's an airy tone to her voice, a sense of ease, almost a giggle in the back of her throat. You know, the type of voice a person has when dirt has never existed under their finger nails.

CAMARO: That New Lenox voice.

ASTON: She calls me, "Sweetie."

CAMARO: Fuck off.

ASTON: She says, "Oh sweetie, it's after midnight. Is everything all right?"

I say, "Have you heard from Emily and Blaise?"

I can hear her smile through the phone as the giggle in the back of her throat moves to the front.

She says, "Oooooohhhh, sweetie, yes, they had a great time at the dance but 'Blaisey' and Emily were very tired. They came home at midnight and I told Emily not to worry. She could stay here for tonight. It's no trouble at all! We have a comfy day-bed in our basement."

CAMARO: Oh fuck.

ASTON: The only thing that happens after midnight with two seventeen year olds in a basement with a day-bed is // pregnancy.

CAMARO: Pregnancy.

ASTON: I call Emily's phone. I don't stop calling 'til she picks up. She answers like she's surprised to hear from me.

CAMARO: She got an excuse ready.

ASTON: Tells me they technically DID get home by midnight, just not her home. She was so tired she forgot to call me. But I don't need to freak out or anything 'cause she's with Blaise, and Kristen, and her date, and Mrs. Bennington (or Bebe 'cause she's cool like that and lets Blaise's friends call her by her first name). Bebe made some fruit punch and cookies. They're all in the basement playing Cards Against Humanity.

CAMARO: You've used that excuse before.

ASTON: Next thing I know, I'm pulling into the Bennington's driveway, park in front of their three car garage, right behind Bebe's new Lexus that Mr. Bennington bought her for Christmas.

CAMARO: What kind of people buy each other cars // for Christmas?

ASTON: NOT OUR PEOPLE! I walk right up to their double doors, but before I could knock, Bebe answers. There she is standing in her matching Chanel track suit, Pandora bracelet dangling off her wrist, and her rock of a wedding ring reflecting her porch lights. It's one in the morning... she still has a full face of makeup on.

CAMARO: And you look like...

Motions to her current state.

ASTON: Bebe has this concerned look grow over her face, but still with that giggle in her throat and says, "Sweetie! Is everything all right?"

I realize she's looking at my scrubs. There's a blood stain and on the upper part of my leg is a large brown spot that is either the chocolate pudding I had for a snack or—

CAMARO: —You had chocolate // pudding?

ASTON: It's been a rough weekend! I try to calm down. Match her tone with that New Lenox ease, that giggle in the back of the throat. But mine comes out more like a croaking frog as I demand to see Emily.

CAMARO: She stays calm.

ASTON: As cool as a God blessed cucumber.

CAMARO: How was the basement?

ASTON: Gorgeous... perfect... more beautiful than my entire house. I would live there and happily pay rent.

CAMARO: And Emily...?

ASTON: There she is, sitting on the day-bed with Blaise... and Kristen... and Kristen's date... drinking fruit punch, eating cookies, and playing Cards Against Humanity.

CAMARO: Oh no... you're the bad guy.

ASTON: I'm the crazy bad guy. If that wasn't bad enough, Emily looked right at me and... That girl has not cried in front of me since she was five years-old, and all of a sudden, right on cue... she. Starts. Balling.

CAMARO: Crocodile tears.

ASTON: I swear to Heavenly Father, I saw her smirk under that stream, and I whispered to myself, "Bitch."

CAMARO: Just like you used to do with Daddy.

ASTON: I'm mush.

CAMARO: Why didn't ya call me yesterday?

ASTON: I have been fielding phone calls all day from Bebe, and Kristen's parents, and Kristen's date's parents 'bout how they're, "shocked," "saddened," "concerned" that I don't trust their children, which means I don't trust them as parents. What kind of parents let their seventeen-year-olds stay out 'til 3 A.M.?

CAMARO: Rich ones, 'cause they can afford the lawyers when their kids screw up.

ASTON: Do you know when Emily started crying, Bebe looked at me with those eyes that whispered, "You poor, dumb little girl. Dunno what you got yourself into." I felt like I was twenty-two again dropping Emily off at kindergarten.

CAMARO: Hey! We don't think 'bout those people no more. What the fuck do they know anyway?

ASTON: They know how to do math. Twenty-two-year-old with a five-year-old.

CAMARO: You weren't THAT much younger than them.

ASTON: In mom years, the distance between a twenty-two-year-old with a five-year-old and a thirty-year-old with a five-year-old is greater than the Grand Canyon. Plus, I look young for my age.

CAMARO: [...]

ASTON: I look young for my age!

CAMARO: Of course!

ASTON: They don't know. None of them do. I had every option, but I chose to keep her.

CAMARO: You had a feelin'.

ASTON: Sometimes those feelings can be wrong. Think that's how your mom felt before she took off?

CAMARO: Some people swerve and some don't.

ASTON: I wish I could just take off. I would always come home, but I just want that "middle of the week" kind of vacation.

CAMARO: You got that secret stash. One day ya can.

ASTON: Five years. It took me five years to save one thousand dollars.

CAMARO: One thousand TEN dollars.

ASTON: What kind of people need five years to save one thousand dollars?

CAMARO: OUR kind of people. People who put themselves through nursin' school, supported their husband through EMT trainin', have a daughter in high school, medical bills for a sick father... and a sister who needed a favor, but couldn't ask.

> Pause.

ASTON: What's family for.

CAMARO: I'm gonna pay you back.

ASTON: You said.

CAMARO: I mean it, Aston. Every last penny. I know what I promised.

ASTON: I'm only concerned with one promise.

> ASTON walks over to the Chevy and places her hands on the car.

CAMARO: I'm workin' on it.

ASTON: I've seen you fix complete, total wrecks in less than a month.

CAMARO: I had Daddy helpin' me. I've never in my life broken a promise to you.

ASTON: I'm not worried 'bout you breaking a promise.

CAMARO: Then what?

ASTON: I gotta feeling. If you don't let this go...

CAMARO: What?

ASTON: This car is gonna tear you and everything apart.

> The bell rings. A customer is waiting.

You should get that.

CAMARO: It's okay. Someone in front will getum.

ASTON: Nick and Marty both here?

CAMARO: Yeah... kinda...

ASTON: In that case, here. Thought I'd never get to drop her off.

> ASTON hands CAMARO her keys.

CAMARO: What's wrong with your car?

ASTON: Whaddya think?

CAMARO: Come on! The headlight?

ASTON: I can't figure it out either. She hits one bump, one tiny, normal crack in the road and she's a pirate again.

CAMARO: Ya might have to take her to a dealer.

ASTON: And have them charge me eight-hundred dollars for a headlight?

CAMARO: Ya got the money.

ASTON: That one thousand and ten dollars is for me. Something special.

CAMARO: I dunno. Not even Daddy could figure it out.

ASTON: Maybe it needs a fresh set of eyes to look at her.

> *LUCKY enters.*

LUCKY: Hey, first customer needs an oil change and tires rotated. Ya wanna handle it? This way I can keep workin' on the cars in the lot, is that cool?

> *Sees ASTON.*

Oh, hi there.

ASTON: Hello?

LUCKY: Didn't see ya come in.

> *LUCKY makes her way to the fridge and grabs a beer.*

ASTON: I came in through the back—

Those are for employees only!

LUCKY: I know...

CAMARO: Aston, don't freak out.

> *LUCKY finds her maintenance jumpsuit on the rack and zips in.*

ASTON: Who is this?

LUCKY: I'm Lucky.

ASTON: Is that some kind of joke?

CAMARO: Her name is Lucy, but she goes by Lucky.

LUCKY: You're her sister?

ASTON: Aston.

LUCKY: Oh, you're all named after cars... is that like a family thing?

ASTON: Who is this!? And why is she drinking a beer?

LUCKY: 'Cause I work here.

CAMARO: Temporarily. Aston, so please, // just don't—

ASTON: Oh no... no, no, no, no! You gotta be kidding me right now! I come to you, come to you as your sister, as your blood, on my hands and knees begging // you...

CAMARO: Ya brought an extra // donut—

ASTON: And this is how you repay me? How you repay family? You give me this speech 'bout not hiring. You got this. This is YOUR garage and you're gonna run things YOUR way. No new employees, no thank you. Not even your own niece! Your own flesh and blood. And now I come in here, not even 72 hours later, to find my ONLY sister has hired some random stranger off // the street.

LUCKY: I'm not exactly a // stranger—

ASTON: Don't you dare interrupt me, girl! The only thing in my veins is contempt and coffee.

CAMARO: Aston, come on, Emily doesn't wanna work here and ya know it! She'd hate it!

ASTON: This must be how Jesus felt when Judas stabbed him in the back.

LUCKY: I think you're thinkin' of Julius Caesar. Judas was a kiss, Brutus stabbed Caesar // in the back—

ASTON: Listen here, girl, two things: one, you do not correct my scripture and two, unless your last name is Gibson or you are somehow married into this family, you got no business being here. This is a FAMILY garage. It's a tradition made by our Daddy—

LUCKY: —Well, then your Dad broke it.

ASTON: Excuse me?

LUCKY: This was like 28 years ago, you guys woulda been kids, right? Your dad did hire outside the family once. His name was James.

CAMARO: No one named James worked here.

LUCKY: You probably woulda known him better as Jay.

ASTON: Oh Lord... Uncle Jay...

LUCKY: Yeah, well, Jay Wells, that was my dad.

CAMARO: How could I forget Uncle Jay?

ASTON: He only worked here for a couple years.

LUCKY: It was two years... then he joined the Marines.

Mr. Gibson always fixed my dad's junker of a car and never charged him. My dad, I dunno, he was a fucked up teenager. Mr. Gibson would tell my dad that his payment was listenin' to his advice. My dad started workin' here when he needed direction and when he found it, he enlisted. I dunno, I'm hopin' this garage can point me in the right direction too.

CAMARO: She's not hired. She's just good with cars, Aston. Even Daddy would like her handy work.

ASTON: She can fix a headlight?

LUCKY: Ya kiddin'? I can have you in and out before you finish your coffee.

ASTON: Meh, this one is halfway done. Camaro, lemme take your car, I'll make another run.

CAMARO tosses ASTON her keys.

ASTON: What kind of donut you like, Lucky?

LUCKY: Chocolate Long Johns.

ASTON: You'll get it IF you fix my headlight before I get back.

ASTON exits.

Lights fade.

End Scene 3.

SCENE 4

Lights up on the garage. It is completely empty except for the Chevy Camaro. It is the evening of Scene 3.

LUCKY enters happily exhausted and hangs up her jumpsuit. She grabs another beer from the fridge and starts to drink. She prepares to exit, but stops short and begins to admire the Chevy. Her admiration leads her to the engine. She gently traces it with her fingertips. She feels the power from the engine radiating through her body. It emboldens her and she hops in the driver's side placing her beer in the console. A smile grows across her face. Her happiness transforms into childish imagination as she pretends to be driving down some highway pushing 120 mph, or perhaps in a drag race. She makes car noises and exaggerated turns. CAMARO enters from the office.

CAMARO: What are you doin'?!

Startled, LUCKY hops out of the car.

LUCKY: Sorry, I was—

CAMARO: —What? Don't touch this car, ya hear me?

LUCKY: Yes, ma'am.

CAMARO: Now, come on, I need a hand.

CAMARO leads LUCKY over to the office door. Camaro quickly unscrews the lock on the door and discards it. She takes a new lock from her jumpsuit pocket and places it in the hole.

Hold it still for me.

LUCKY does as CAMARO screws in the new lock. She takes a key out of her pocket and tests it to make sure it works.

LUCKY: Office got broken into?

CAMARO: We just got some snoops.

CAMARO puts the key back in her pocket.

LUCKY: Do I get a key or...

CAMARO: I never missed a day of work in my life.

LUCKY: Got it.

Beat.

Thank you.

CAMARO: For what?

LUCKY: Takin' a chance on me. I guess that sorta thing runs in your family.

CAMARO: My sister will be the first to tell ya I ain't good at askin' for help. But ya helped me, so ya can keep showin' up if ya want, but you get this straight in your head, this is conditional, understand? I'll call when I need ya, pay ya in cash, and ya can drink my beer, but that don't make you a Gibson.

LUCKY: Do you guys really get by with just the three of ya?

CAMARO: There's always another cousin needin' work. Whether it's three months, six months, or a year. My mom had a big family and I just ride their waves of guilt.

LUCKY: I take it Aston doesn't have a knack for cars.

CAMARO: Nah, she's got a gentle hand. Can't be that way with cars, they're machines, they only listen to tough love. Now, I fix cars and she fixes people.

LUCKY: Praise the Lord—

CAMARO: —Don't make fun. All that Jesus talk got her through when she found out she was pregnant. Now, its all fate, destiny, and "I gotta feelin'." I dunno, she was a lost girl, just like my niece. Now, she got direction and believes she's part of some big plan. God puts people where He needs them or whatever.

LUCKY: Ya don't believe that?

CAMARO: Nah. I think ya make your own way. People come into your life by chance. Not some master plan. Ya make your choices, those choices have outcomes. Ya just try not to fuck people over. If you make a commitment, you honor it. You don't swerve.

LUCKY: I get it. But um, if I'm gonna be comin' here, I feel like I gotta know some things, first.

CAMARO: Oh?

LUCKY: Look, I'm here to fix cars and I'm gonna do a damn good job for ya. It's the least I can do for everythin' Mr. Gibson did for my dad so, you don't gotta worry 'bout me sayin' anythin'.

CAMARO: Whaddya gettin' at?

LUCKY: When Aston paid me for the part for her car she gave me a credit card... It said Denise on it. Now, like I said, I ain't gonna say shit. It's none of my business. I'm here to fix cars and that's exactly what I'll say to anyone that comes around, but I just gotta know if there's somethin' goin' on that I "shouldn't know 'bout..." Know what I mean?

CAMARO: Damn, ya get that loyalty from the Marines?

LUCKY: You look out for the guy on your six.

CAMARO: I guess if I ever need to move a dead body I know who to call. At ease, Sergeant. We ain't runnin' scams here. Aston's name is Denise. Her parents died when she was little. My mom, with the last good bone in her body, took her in. She was my mom's sister's kid. When she got a li'l older, she wanted to feel like she was apart of our family. My daddy renamed her Aston, and that's that.

LUCKY: So, it's like a nickname?

CAMARO: No, her name is Aston Gibson. She is my only sister. No one except government papers calls her Denise, ya hear me?

LUCKY: Loud and clear.

CAMARO: Ya know, I'm usually the last one here.

LUCKY: That's alright, I live just a couple blocks down on 64th and Lawndale.

CAMARO: That's right around the corner. Easy to get home to your family.

LUCKY: It's just me. I live in my old house. My dad left it to me.

CAMARO: Wow, house all to yourself.

LUCKY: It's just a big, empty space, it's not a home. Just empty. Know what I mean?

> *Pause. CAMARO takes a wad of cash out of her pocket, counts it, and hands it to LUCKY.*

CAMARO: I'll call ya if I need ya tomorrow.

> *LUCKY takes the money.*

LUCKY: Do ya need help lockin' up?

CAMARO: No, when it's quiet like this I get to work on the Chevy.

LUCKY: Okay.

CAMARO: I prefer to do it alone.

> *LUCKY gets It. She unzips from her jumpsuit and exits. CAMARO watches her go and locks the door behind her. Camaro approaches the Chevy, reaches into her jumpsuit, and pulls out a piston ring.*

Just a thin, metal ring.

> *She fixes the piston ring in the engine, then goes over to a box on the work station. She opens the box and takes out a vintage steering wheel. She gets into the Chevy with some tools and screws the steering wheel into place. CAMARO reaches into the glove compartment and pulls out the keys.*
>
> *Pause.*
>
> *CAMARO starts the car. The engine revs. Camaro sits for a moment clutching the steering wheel. She is unsatisfied. It is not a heartbeat. She shuts off the car. She gets out and heads for the engine. She takes the same piston ring out of the engine and places it back in her jumpsuit.*

Maybe tomorrow, your heart will beat.

> *Lights begin to fade.*
>
> *End of Scene 4.*

SCENE 5

Lights up on the garage. It is the evening of Thanksgiving. In addition to the steering wheel, the Chevy now has a windshield. ASTON enters from the outside door in her nursing scrubs.

ASTON: Hello...? Lucky...?

> *Pause. No answer. She immediately heads to the office door. She tries her key that no longer works. She roughly jiggles the handle and then gives up.*

(*Frustrated to herself*)

Camaro...

> *LUCKY enters from swinging door wearing her jumpsuit carrying a tire iron ready to fight an intruder.*

LUCKY: I'm 'bout to light your ass up! Oh! Aston, it's just you.

ASTON: At ease! Camaro pay you for guard duty too?

LUCKY: Uh, Camaro changed the lock last month.

ASTON: I see that. Guess she forgot to tell me.

LUCKY: I can ask her to make ya a key—

ASTON: —No, no... don't bring it up. It's just, sister things. She's been forgetful before. We'll keep this one between you and me.

LUCKY: Cool.

ASTON: What are you doing here on Thanksgiving?

LUCKY: I asked Camaro earlier this week if I could come in today to get through these cars.

ASTON: Yeah, Camaro told me 'bout that. She gave you your own key?

LUCKY: Nah, just lent me hers

ASTON: Wow, maybe my prayers have been working. There's hope for you yet.

LUCKY: I dunno, we've been gettin' slammed and I could use some cash for the holidays.

ASTON: Work has definitely been picking up. People tend to trust places they know are reliable.

LUCKY: Makes sense.

ASTON: Camaro is the same way. Dependability is what makes you a Gibson.

LUCKY: Got it.

ASTON: So, you heading to Thanksgiving dinner now or...

LUCKY: Oh, I don't really have much family left, just my uncle and we're not much of cooks. Besides, he's gotta start his shift at Walmart. Black Friday.

ASTON: Did Camaro know this and still not invite you over for Thanksgiving?

LUCKY: I haven't had a Thanksgiving dinner since my dad died. And even then, it was just a turkey and swiss sandwich. The cars keep me company.

ASTON: Cars aren't people. Here. I was gonna have it on my break but I won't be able to digest it knowing you didn't have a Thanksgiving dinner.

> *ASTON takes out some Tupperware.*

LUCKY: It's really okay...

ASTON: No, please, you're doing me a favor. It's Aunt Rita's stuffing. Delicious, but I'm supposed to be on the Keto diet.

> *LUCKY takes the food.*

You got time to take a look at this waste of space? Maybe the Chevy can use some of your luck to make it rev.

LUCKY: No, Camaro made it very clear not to touch.

ASTON: Really?

LUCKY: It's a gorgeous car. It's legendary. I would like to help but—

> *ASTON mimes opening the nonexistent door on the Chevy.*

ASTON: Get in.

LUCKY: Oh... no, I really shoudn't—

ASTON: —He was my daddy too. This is as much my car as it is Camaro's.

LUCKY: Aston, I can't. Camaro would never lemme come back.

ASTON: Oh, I dunno... I feel like forgetfulness can be contagious. My sister forgot to tell me 'bout the new lock, I can forget to tell her 'bout this.

LUCKY: Whatever's goin' on between you and your sister... I don't wanna cause a problem.

ASTON: Look, Lucky, I gotta feeling 'bout you. Your dad helped my daddy and now you're helping my sister, whether she likes to admit it or not. It's Thanksgiving. You should be with people making memories around a dinner table. We don't have a dinner table here, but we have this car.

> *LUCKY slides into the car. ASTON walks around to the passenger side and loudly clears her throat.*

You gonna lemme in?

LUCKY: Oh, uh, sure...?

> *LUCKY reaches over and pretends to unlock the imaginary door.*

ASTON: Put your hands on the wheel. Go ahead...

What's the first thing you do when you get into a car?

LUCKY: Huh... check my mirrors?

ASTON: Go ahead.

LUCKY: Ya don't got any.

ASTON: Close your eyes.

> *LUCKY does.*

It's a 1967 Chevy Camaro. No buttons to adjust anything. Everything is by hand.

LUCKY: Okay...?

> *ASTON closes her eyes.*

ASTON: I think your side mirror needs adjusting. Do you see it now?

LUCKY: Yeah, yeah I do.

> *LUCKY keeps her eyes closed and hands on the wheel throughout the entire exchange. She imagines adjusting the mirror.*

Just need to push it out a bit... there. Now I can see.

ASTON: Lemme check my hair in the rearview.

> *ASTON's hands do not move from her lap. LUCKY still has her eyes closed.*

LUCKY: You look great.

ASTON: Now what?

LUCKY: Seat belts.

ASTON: Of course.

LUCKY: Then I start the car.

> *Silence.*

ASTON: Hear that engine?

LUCKY: Roars like a dragon.

> *Silence.*

What station we listenin' to?

ASTON: This is your drive, not mine.

LUCKY: Alright. There we go. Rotting Christ.

ASTON: Seriously?

LUCKY: You said it was my drive.

ASTON: Alright, alright.

> *ASTON makes the sign of the cross.*

Where are we?

LUCKY: Just got on I-5 North from Basilone Road.

ASTON: Where?

LUCKY: Shhh? Ya don't hear it? It's in the distance now, but ya can still hear the boots on the ground. "Left, right, left. Left, right, left.

LUCKY (CONT'D): Fall in. Present arms. Port arms. High port arms. Order arms." Ya do what your told. Ya do what ya know.

ASTON: We can leave that behind. What's on the road around us?

LUCKY: Look to your left. Ever see the Pacific Ocean before?

> *ASTON breathes in deep trying to smell the salt.*

ASTON: I'm trying to smell it.

LUCKY: She's gonna guide us the whole way there. San Clemente, Laguna Beach, Newport Beach—

ASTON: —I heard they got some good shopping there.

LUCKY: Don't got time for a pit stop. Gotta be back to base by seventeen hundred hours.

ASTON: Then you better step on it.

LUCKY: 405-North. We're close.

ASTON: We'll get there. This car has driven up and down that coast a few times.

LUCKY: Sunset Boulevard to Bellagio Drive.

ASTON: Where are we?

LUCKY: UCLA.

ASTON: It's warm.

LUCKY: It's perfect.

> *ASTON opens her eyes and stares at LUCKY dreaming of UCLA's campus.*

ASTON: You go to school there?

> *LUCKY's eyes snap open. She releases her grip from the steering wheel.*

LUCKY: Uh, no. I was stationed in Pendleton, 'bout two hours away.

ASTON: You know the drive.

LUCKY: I got the crazy idea to visit from my gunnery sergeant. He saw me fix tank after tank, machine after machine. Eight years in motor T; ya do what ya know. I'm good with my hands. Machines are like puzzles. Ya just gotta find the missin' piece. I told him, I said, "Gunny, gimme somethin' hard. I don't wannna fix things that are broken. I wanna design things so they don't break in the first place."

ASTON: That's ambitious.

LUCKY: That's an engineer. Eight years, I was a terminal sergeant, but I wasn't ready to go home yet. Somethin' was keepin' me there.

ASTON: You gotta feeling.

LUCKY: Gunny said to go on up to the campus and say hello to a Professor Hamlin for him.

ASTON: Who's that?

LUCKY: She's a professor in the Mechanical Engineering department... and former Marine. That entire campus looked like polished metal. I didn't wanna shake her hand. I never realized how dirty my hands were.

ASTON: Nothing wrong with a little dirt.

LUCKY: No one in my family went to college and who am I to break that tradition? It's not off the #54 bus or the orange line I got no business bein' there. "If ya ain't sweatin', ya ain't workin'."

ASTON: Your dad?

LUCKY: Yeah.

ASTON: Yeah, your dad definitely hung around mine. "Gibsons create with our hands. We fix things other people can't."

LUCKY: He called me Lucky 'cause I was his Lucky "Loosey." The last cigarette ya didn't know ya had.

ASTON: Sounds like he loved you.

LUCKY: Said he wouldn't survive without me... and he didn't.

> *Pause.*

ASTON: This garage is blessed. It has the power to make people feel like they belong. Like they're home.

LUCKY: Well, only if Camaro lets ya in.

ASTON: Do you believe in fate?

LUCKY: I dunno, I mean, no offense, I dunno if I believe in God or whatever, but the universe... In the Marines, they teach ya to focus on somethin' that is greater than yourself; the big picture, ya know? I'm nuthin' without the guy on my six, and he's nuthin' without me, and that's how the entire platoon functions. We're all connected. Maybe ya meet people by chance, but it's what ya do when ya meet them that sets a bigger plan in motion.

ASTON: I want you to do something for me, well, it's really for Camaro, but she'll be too stubborn to realize it.

LUCKY: Anythin'.

ASTON: You said you like to put broken things back together. I want you to help put this car back together.

LUCKY: Aston, if Camaro were to hear 'bout me just sittin' here, she would lose her shit.

ASTON: I'll talk to her.

LUCKY: She's makin' progress... slowly.

ASTON: Very. Slowly.

LUCKY: I don't wanna lose what I barely have.

ASTON: You won't. I'll make sure of it.

LUCKY: How do you know?

ASTON: Who do you think convinced her to give you the key for today? Dependability makes you a Gibson. You help with this car, I'll make sure you can call this place home for as long as you want.

LUCKY: Lemme do it my way.

ASTON: What does that mean?

LUCKY: Please. I don't want anythin' handed to me. I wanna earn this.

ASTON: I knew I had a feeling 'bout you.

> *Lights fade.*
>
> *End Scene 5.*

SCENE 6

Lights up on the garage. It's December 23rd. CAMARO is working on the Chevy. ASTON is sitting in the car scrolling through her phone. Text message pings are heard. Aston purposefully ignores them and continues to scroll.

ASTON: Do you think my first designer purchase should be Fendi or Blahnik?

The sound of text message pinging continues.

CAMARO: I dunno what those words mean.

Ping.

ASTON: "Oh, why hello, Bebe, didn't even notice you were here. Why yes! These are the latest collection from Fendi. Quite exclusive, but I wouldn't dare be caught a season behind. Your shoes are lovely too, I think I saw them in last summer's JC Penny's catalogue"

Ping. Ping.

CAMARO: Ya gonna get that?

ASTON: Emily is just writing her manifesto 'bout how unfair her life is.

CAMARO: I'm proud of ya. I'd thought ya'd cave.

ASTON: No New Lenox, no basement, and no Blaise for all of Christmas break if she does not finish her college applications.

Ping. Ping. Ping.

CAMARO: Ya know, Moraine Valley ain't that bad.

ASTON: It's a community college.

CAMARO: So?

ASTON: There's nothing wrong with Moraine, but I know the only reason she wants to go there is 'cause of that boy.

LUCKY excitedly enters.

CAMARO: Lucky! Whaddya doin' here?

ASTON: How's your uncle?

LUCKY: Not much better. I told him to take it easy after Black Friday. But, "if ya ain't sweatin', ya ain't workin'." His back is pretty busted.

CAMARO: Sorry to hear that, but I got it covered here. It's the day before Christmas Eve, go home.

ASTON: Before you go, tell me, do you think Fendi or Blahnik for my Christmas gift? Oh! What 'bout Louboutins!?

LUCKY: I dunno what those words mean, but I have a Christmas present for you, Camaro. Hold on...

LUCKY exits. Ping. Ping. Ping.

ASTON: Did you get that girl anything?

CAMARO: Is Emily writin' a book?

ASTON: Camaro!

CAMARO: I gave her the week off....

Ping. Ping. Ping.

Don't look at me like that and turn it off if ya ain't gonna answer.

ASTON turns off her phone.

ASTON: Camaro, it's not right. Daddy wouldn't do this. He treated Uncle Jay like family.

CAMARO: I'll figure somethin' out, okay?

Tires begin rolling in from offstage. LUCKY follows behind.

LUCKY: Merry Christmas!

ASTON: Oh my Lord...

LUCKY: Wasn't easy findin' the tires and the rims, they might be comin' later. I'm still lookin', but my guy might know a guy.

CAMARO: These are for the Chevy?

ASTON: This must of cost you a fortune.

LUCKY: Oh, nah. My guy, he served and now he runs a junkyard. He goes to a lot of those antique car shows and helps put cars together. He lemme use my "military" discount.

ASTON: Thank you. Ahem... Camaro?

CAMARO: You didn't have to do this, Lucky.

LUCKY: No big deal. I know a guy, who knows a guy... The country doesn't do shit for vets so, we look out for each other. Besides, the least I can do is give this baby some shoes. It's snowin' and he looked cold.

CAMARO: I dunno what to say?

ASTON: Well, maybe there's nothing to say. Just something to do. Go on, tie up the shoe laces.

CAMARO nods her head and rolls a tire into position.

ASTON: I think it'd be a lot easier with two people. Lucky, do you mind helping out? I gotta squeeze in a nap before my night class starts.

CAMARO: No, I can do // it—

ASTON: I remember you telling me Daddy would admire her handy work.

Beat.

CAMARO: Lucky, it'll go a lot faster with two of us.

ASTON: See you on Christmas, Big Sister. Lucky, in case Camaro forgets, you're welcome over to my house too.

LUCKY smiles as ASTON exits. Lucky approaches the tire.

Pause.

CAMARO and LUCKY lock eyes.

CAMARO: Let's get somethin' straight: you're gonna touch the body of the car and only the body of the car, hear me?

LUCKY: Yes ma'am.

CAMARO: If your guy keeps gettin' more parts, you can help install them AFTER I approve them and ONLY if they're for the body.

LUCKY: Yes ma'am.

CAMARO: You see that engine? That engine belonged to my Daddy's 1967 Chevy Camaro. He chased my Mom all the way from oceanside California, down Route 66 to Chicago in it. 'Cause that's what a Camaro does. It chases things. But he got stuck here 'cause of me, so he couldn't chase no more. Car lost its purpose. Heart lost its beat and the body got torn up and rusted away. But you do not get to touch the heart, hear me?

LUCKY: Yes ma'am.

CAMARO: Now help me with this tire.

LUCKY helps position the tire on the Chevy.

LUCKY: You don't gotta worry 'bout me, Camaro.

CAMARO: I'm still tryin' to decide if you're a swerver or not. I got no time for that, hear me? I got enough people comin' in, goin' out, turnin' left instead of right and leavin' at the drop of a hat. So, if you're a swerver, don't bullshit me.

LUCKY: I got your six.

CAMARO: Ooo fuckin' rah.

CAMARO gets the speed drill and locks eyes with LUCKY.

Pause.

Thank you.

Speed drill sounds as CAMARO installs the tire.

Lights fade.

End Scene 6.

SCENE 7

Lights up on the garage. It is close to midnight on New Year's Eve. The Chevy sits as we last saw with all four tires, but now one door has been installed. LUCKY is busy installing the other door. She stands back and admires her work. ASTON enters from the outside.

LUCKY: The office is still locked.

ASTON: I know my sister. I'm not worried. Camaro give you your own set of keys?

LUCKY: Just lent me hers. Don't think I'll ever get my own set.

ASTON: It's almost midnight on New Year's Eve, you should be out celebrating.

LUCKY: See for yourself...

LUCKY motions to the Chevy's new doors.

ASTON: Oh my...

LUCKY: Look.

LUCKY opens the passenger side door for ASTON and ushers her in. Aston smiles and slides in as Lucky shuts the car door.

No more pretend.

ASTON opens and closes the door a few times in disbelief. She then reaches over and unlocks the driver's side door.

ASTON: Get in. It's negative 5 outside and I would like to take a tour of the UCLA campus.

LUCKY: Nah, that's okay. I don't need to go back.

ASTON: It's never too late.

LUCKY: I dunno, I sat in on Professor Hamlin's class and it was just... I was twenty-five and sittin' with a bunch of eighteen-year olds that were already far ahead of me. It doesn't seem like that big of an age gap but it felt like—

ASTON: —The Grand Canyon. You know, Lucky, I started late too, but I'm a few years older than you and I'm still going.

LUCKY: If it's not off the orange line or the #54, I got no business bein' there.

ASTON: You told me you had a feeling that drew you to that campus.

LUCKY: No one in my family has ever left the Southside of Chicago, unless we're dressed in our fatigues. I sat in the back of that class and watched Professor Hamlin talkin' 'bout designs, her projects, the things she's buildin' that'll never break. But, come on, Aston, what kind of girl from West Lawn, with dirt under her nails, goes to California?

ASTON: Where does a girl from West Lawn go?

LUCKY: We stick to bus routes and the orange line. I worked at Walmart for two years before I came here.

ASTON: How's your uncle doing?

LUCKY: I keep tellin' him, "Walmart will kill you, just like it killed dad." They both went from sergeants in the Marines to stackin' boxes on a shelf for $8.25 an hour.

ASTON: Sounds like you want more.

LUCKY: At first, I enlisted for my dad. The first few years when I came home on leave, I would do these exhibition drills for him...

> *LUCKY picks up a tire iron and starts to do a basic drill for ASTON.*

ASTON: I never understood the point of those.

LUCKY: Discipline. Shows ya know how to follow orders and fall into formation. Ya do what ya know. Ya do what you're told.

ASTON: You don't strike me as someone who follows.

LUCKY: I got selfish.

ASTON: How?

LUCKY: Somethin' changed. I wasn't his daughter no more; I wasn't some girl from West Lawn, I was a Marine Corps sergeant standin' on a beach in California. I reenlisted and stayed for as long as I could. But then, my dad begged me to come home. He said, "Eight years and a terminal sergeant, my service is done."

ASTON: What was Professor Hamlin like?

LUCKY: A marine through and through. Hard to believe though. She shined like everythin' else on that campus. But all my dad said was, "We ain't college people, don't be selfish. This family can't survive without ya." I got the news and came home. They said heart attack; too old to be stackin' boxes, but nowhere else would take him. I coulda helped him and I wouldn't be comin' home to an empty house.

ASTON: This garage is pretty full.

LUCKY: I'm not a Gibson.

ASTON: You sure? Camaro leave you a Second Christmas present?

LUCKY: No...?

> *ASTON reaches into her bag and pulls out a pair of thermal socks.*

ASTON: Thermal socks. It gets cold in the garage during the winter.

And... where would she hide mine?

> *ASTON starts searching the garage for something. LUCKY, confused but curious, watches her.*

LUCKY: What are ya lookin' for?

ASTON continues her search while she speaks.

ASTON: It was the first Christmas after Camaro's mom left. The day after Christmas me and Camaro would go over by our friends' houses and would see the piles and piles of toys they got from Santa. That year, we only got maybe two each. So, on New Year's Day our daddy brought us here and said Santa told him since we were extra special this year, he found some more presents in his sleigh and hid them somewhere in the shop for us. No one else in the neighborhood got an extra present from Santa. They weren't as special as us Gibson girls.

ASTON has a light bulb moment and goes to the Chevy. She opens the glove compartment and pulls out a small, white box with a red bow taped on top.

Come on, Camaro! I specifically told you not to—

LUCKY: —What is it?

ASTON opens the box.

ASTON: Rocky road fudge and a key.

ASTON sighs, but then takes half of the fudge and shoves it in her mouth.

I guess I can start my diet tomorrow. Resolutions, you know. Now, only half of this will tempt me. Don't tell her.

LUCKY: What's the key for?

ASTON places the box back in the glove compartment. She walks over to the office door.

ASTON: It's not supposed to be anything big. Socks, chocolate...

She unlocks the office door.

Or an apology.

ASTON looks for a place to hide the socks. She settles on behind the counter.

You should look for yours.

LUCKY: So, does Emily still buy into the whole Second Christmas, or is she "so over" Santa.

ASTON: She'll be here tomorrow and she'll find... this!

ASTON pulls out a large binder with a bow taped on top.

LUCKY: Homework...?

ASTON: I printed it off the internet. It's a directory of almost every college and university in the U.S. with brief descriptions of their majors, and most importantly, their application deadlines— which I highlighted the ones I want her to look at.

She hands LUCKY the binder who begins to flip through the pages.

LUCKY: Wow...

ASTON: Emily only submitted one application. A lot of the deadlines have lapsed, but there are still some that aren't due 'til mid-February.

LUCKY: Where'd she apply?

ASTON: Well, I helped her with ISU 'cause // Kristen is probably going there.

LUCKY: It's a big party school.

ASTON: What?

LUCKY: It's really great for teachin', too.

ASTON: She's also been talking 'bout going to Moraine. Which is a great community college, but I know she only wants to go 'cause of—

LUCKY: —Blaise.

ASTON: Yeah...

LUCKY: Well, I think it's a great gift, but Emily might equate this to a lump of coal.

ASTON: Which is why Santa also got her...

Reaches into her bag.

Twenty-dollar gift card to Forever 21. Which I will hide toward the end of this, so she has to flip through the pages to find it.

ASTON tucks the card away. LUCKY looks at the opened page a little stunned.

LUCKY: Uh... you highlighted Harvard.

ASTON: Yeah. Also Yale, Princeton, Brown—

LUCKY: —No offense, but are ya fuckin' crazy?

ASTON: Look at me, I'm wearing seven-year-old shoes with stains all over my scrubs that I hope to God is NOT fecal matter. I know we're not Harvard people, or Princeton people, or Yale people... Our people work with our hands, not our wallets. But every now and then, God helps one of us slip through those Ivy cracks. And when we do, we show them what our sweat and dirty hands can do. Why can't it be Emily? Why can't it be anyone? Even a girl from West Lawn?

LUCKY: I thought I was helpin' ya here?

ASTON: You are, more than you know, but if God thinks it's meant to be, it'll be. I mean, if Harvard takes Emily... like hell we got the money, but we would figure it out. That's what you do when God opens a crack for you. It's not being selfish to look out for yourself. Trust me, you don't wanna swerve at the last minute.

LUCKY: The application fees are like crazy expensive, right? Fifty, seventy-five, a hundred dollars some of them... I can't fuckin' afford that right now.

>*Pause. ASTON takes out her checkbook and writes. She tears out a check and hands it to LUCKY.*

ASTON: Here.

>*LUCKY takes the check.*

LUCKY: A hundred dollars?! Aston, no! Please... I can't take this.

ASTON: Yes, you can.

LUCKY: No, really, this is too much-

ASTON: —It's okay. I got some extra money saved up. A secret stash. You take that and you apply. Just trying can be your Second Christmas gift to me.

LUCKY: Second Christmas is supposed to be small. Socks, chocolate...

ASTON: Well, I didn't get you a Christmas gift either so... merry Christmas and merry Second Christmas.

>*Notices the time.*

Oh, and happy New Year.

Hide that in the office for Emily when you're done looking.

>*ASTON exits.*

>*LUCKY flips through the binder's pages as she makes her way to the mini fridge. She opens the fridge and pulls out a tiny wrapped package; her Second Christmas present from CAMARO. She opens the package to reveal a set of keys. She tries the keys on the outside door of the shop. They work. She holds the gift in one hand and the binder in the other.*

>*Lights fade.*

>*End Scene 7.*

SCENE 8

Lights up on the garage. It's the middle of March, St. Patrick's Day. The Chevy Camaro is just missing the hood over the engine. One half of the car looks like some paint colors were tested. The other half is an old-fashioned sky blue. CAMARO is on the sky blue side of the car with a paint gun. She examines her work and is pleased. ASTON comes bursting through the door, full of energy.

ASTON: SHE DID IT! She did it! Sweet Jesus, thank you! She did it!

CAMARO: Start celebratin' early, have we?

ASTON: You wanna go out? Lawlors? I'll buy, the whole day! I got the money saved!

CAMARO: On St. Patrick's Day? I'm not goin' anywhere near a Southside Irish bar. And that money is somethin' special FOR YOU. Treat yourself to a weekend downtown. Sleep in one of those fancy king-sized hotel beds.

ASTON: I feel like I could work another shift! This is just... are you ready?

CAMARO: For...?

ASTON: U of I, ISU, Western, Northern, and Madison—

CAMARO: —Wisconsin?

ASTON: Why not? We like cheese! All of them, every single one of them took Emily.

CAMARO: So, no Moraine?

ASTON: She's going, Camaro. She's going far, far away from basements, and Bebe, and Blaise.

CAMARO: Cheers.

ASTON: Gimme a beer.

CAMARO: Seriously?

ASTON: It's St. Patrick's Day, the Whole30 diet doesn't count today.

> *CAMARO goes to the fridge and tosses ASTON an Old Style. She takes one for herself.*

CAMARO: To Emily.

ASTON: And God.

CAMARO: Sure.

> *They clink cans and drink. LUCKY enters from the outside door.*

Hey! You're late, it's almost 10 o'clock.

LUCKY: Sorry.

ASTON: Let 'er go. You're not gonna have any business today. Everyone's already drunk.

CAMARO: You okay?

LUCKY: Yeah.

> *LUCKY puts on her jumpsuit.*

ASTON: Well, we are celebrating!

> *ASTON goes to the fridge and tosses LUCKY a can of beer.*

CAMARO: Emily's out of the basement.

LUCKY: Oh...?

ASTON: U of I, ISU, Western, Northern, Madison... I can keep saying that over and over again. She got in!

LUCKY: That's great!

ASTON: Today is just a blessed day! Emily has options, spring is right around the corner—

CAMARO: —It's 30 degrees with a chance of snow.

ASTON: Perfect day! And look, look at this car!

CAMARO: Be careful! The paint is still a li'l fresh.

ASTON: It's starting to look more and more like Daddy's car.

LUCKY: Nice color blue.

ASTON: Like the California sky.

CAMARO: And his eyes.

ASTON: Today could be the day.

CAMARO: Ya gotta feelin'?

ASTON: I got all types of feelings! Only good things can happen to today.

CAMARO: Well, Daddy did love St. Patty's Day.

ASTON: Only time he could drink in the morning and not be judged.

CAMARO: Let's see if he'll rev.

> *ASTON excitedly runs to the car. LUCKY prepares to exit.*

LUCKY: Any car ya want me to handle first?

CAMARO: There's a Toyota Camry— ya know what...? Nah, nobody's here. They're already at the bars.

> *CAMARO opens the passenger door for LUCKY.*

Get in.

ASTON: Camaro...

LUCKY: What?

CAMARO: I dunno, today's Daddy's favorite holiday and this car, it's startin' to look just like how I remembered him. You helped do that. This space doesn't feel empty, it feels like he's here. So, get in before I change my mind.

LUCKY hesitates then gets in the car. ASTON follows after and makes a loud throat clearing noise.

LUCKY: Oh, sorry...

LUCKY reaches across and unlocks the driver's side door. CAMARO gets in. LUCKY is slightly squished in the middle. ASTON hands her the keys.

CAMARO: To the beginnin' of the end.

ASTON: The end AND the beginning.

ASTON & CAMARO: Old Style sittin' in the console

Wind blowin' through the window

When the rubber meets the concrete

Ya get down on your knees

Pray for your shot

Grab life by the balls and give it all ya got.

They spit. CAMARO turns the key. All three WOMEN close their eyes. The engine chokes, sputters, and dies.

ASTON: Lord....

They all exit the car.

LUCKY: Sorry 'bout that.

ASTON: But I had a feeling...

CAMARO: Maybe God got his wires crossed.

The bell rings. A customer is waiting.

So much for a slow day. Don't touch the engine, I'll be right back.

CAMARO exits out the swinging door.

ASTON: Soooo...?

LUCKY: Yeah?

ASTON: How are you?

LUCKY: Fine.

ASTON: No news to share?

LUCKY: Not really—

ASTON: —Look, I figured you didn't want people asking 'bout it so I kept my mouth shut but... you should of got an email by now.

LUCKY: Oh...

ASTON: I'm just checking on my investment.

LUCKY: Yeah…

ASTON: Good or bad, I just wanna know, I won't tell anyone.

LUCKY: Um, yeah, I got an email from UCLA this mornin'.

ASTON: Oh my God! And…?

LUCKY: Waitlisted.

ASTON: Okay… okay, waitlist, that's not a no—

LUCKY: —I'm not goin'.

ASTON: What? What do you mean—

LUCKY: —I just wanted to try, right? See if I could.

ASTON: Okay, yes: You could, you did, now you take the next step.

LUCKY: The next step involves a lot of movin' parts.

ASTON: When God opens a door for you—

LUCKY: —He opened a door. But he's not exactly footin' the bill.

ASTON: You're a vet. The military helps you with stuff like this. You should take advantage of your hard work. God is rewarding you—

LUCKY: —Can you stop! I'm sorry, I didn't mean—

Look, the last time I left home, my dad died, and I came back to nuthin'. Just an empty house, not a home. Camaro gave me a home again. I told her, I got her six. If it's not off the #54 bus or the orange line, I got no business bein' there.

ASTON: Your dad used to come to my daddy for advice. Now, I'm gonna give you some: you don't owe us a God damn thing.

LUCKY: What?

ASTON: You have such a limited amount of time in this life to be selfish and do what you want to do. If you wait too long you wind up stuck and you got to sit there and pray for an opportunity, for God to open a window just a crack and that window isn't the easiest thing to open. It takes all your muscle, all your energy to swerve left, instead of right. Don't wait for a jammed window. He's holding the door open for you.

LUCKY: I thought you wanted me to help her.

ASTON: You've done your duty. Look at this car. We could drive it outta here today if it wasn't for that godforsaken engine. I dunno, maybe the heart will never beat. But that don't mean you gotta put your life on hold.

CAMARO reenters.

CAMARO: Hey! I got a Honda Accord in the second garage that won't start. I can use some of your luck, Sergeant.

LUCKY: Comin'.

LUCKY and CAMARO exit.
Lights fade on ASTON.
End of Scene 8.

SCENE 9

Lights up on the garage. Later that night of Scene 8. It's empty, except for the Chevy. LUCKY enters from the swinging door still in her jumpsuit. She goes to the work table and begins to put tools away. She starts to unzip, but then rethinks it. She zips back up and stands at attention. She grabs a tire iron and begins to do a military exhibition drill. She repeats the drill over and over again, working herself up, until she flings the tire iron and it hits the Chevy.

LUCKY: Fuck me!

She checks the paint. It's all right. She traces the outline of the car with her eyes closed. As she traces, we hear the sound of military drills and marching mixed with a Walmart speaker system. She traces the car all the way to the engine. The sounds build to a deafening climax and forces LUCKY to grab the engine with both hands.

Then suddenly just the sound of ocean waves on a beach.

LUCKY opens her eyes and takes her hands immediately off the engine, but not before she notices something. She touches the engine. She knows something is missing.

Lights fade.

End of Scene 9.

SCENE 10

Lights up on the garage. It is the beginning of May. CAMARO finishes polishing the now completed Chevy Camaro. It is gorgeous and sparkles in fresh sky blue paint. ASTON is mid-conversation.

ASTON: I told her no. Absolutely not! As long as she is spending my money... // nuh uh nope.

CAMARO: How bad could // it of been?

ASTON: Every dress she picked out made her look like a Vegas showgirl. Did you know that girls aren't wearing long dresses to prom anymore?

CAMARO: I didn't wear a long dress to prom.

ASTON: You wore pants.

CAMARO: I like pants.

ASTON: You wore pants to make fun of prom.

CAMARO: I wore pants 'cause I like pants.

ASTON: Well, I just can't believe it. She's not going, I swear, I won't let her go.

> *LUCKY enters. ASTON hands Lucky her Long John donut from the Dunkin' Donuts bag.*

LUCKY: What did Emily do now?

ASTON: Her prom dress. Everything either had her breasts out or she couldn't even bend over without someone seeing her // whoo-ha.

CAMARO: Do you remember your dream // prom dress, Aston?

ASTON: Lucky, what did you wear to prom?

LUCKY: I didn't go.

CAMARO: Smart // girl.

ASTON: Oh, that's a shame.

LUCKY: I survived. But I guess for my class, it was when the Kardashians were gettin' big so, everyone had like form-fittin' dresses to show off their asses.

ASTON: I pray everyday for these young women.

CAMARO: Fuckin' bullshit! Lemme tell ya 'bout this woman's perfect prom dress. The one she could not live without. Spaghetti strap, cherry red, floor length that hugged every curve, with a slit all the way up her thigh to her hip.

ASTON: It was classic.

CAMARO: For a stroll on the Vegas Strip.

ASTON: Well, I didn't get to wear it, did I?

> *Pause.*

LUCKY: Why not?

Silence.

CAMARO and ASTON share a moment. Aston's eyes cradle shame. The same shame she felt at twenty-two years old, dropping Emily off at kindergarten; Camaro knows her sister.

ASTON: I couldn't-

CAMARO *(more for Aston than Lucky)*: —She had a feelin'.

> *Beat.*

ASTON: God had other plans for me at seventeen.

CAMARO: It wasn't like we could afford the dress anyways. It was kinda expensive.

ASTON: I remember I saw the dress in the fall of my senior year. It was love at first sight.

CAMARO: Poor Steve.

ASTON: Don't listen to "pants" over here. For some people, all it takes is a dress to remind them of who they really are. The Cinderella moment. Daddy gave me fifty bucks.

CAMARO: He didn't know no better. Besides, that's all you should spend on a dress you're only gonna wear once.

ASTON: No, that Cinderella moment is priceless. I tried it on and threw up in a trashcan in the fitting room. I used that fifty to help buy a pregnancy test.

> *Beat.*

LUCKY: Prom's overrated anyways.

ASTON: I want Emily to find her Cinderella dress for her Cinderella moment. And now we're running out of time. It's already May and prom is in three weeks.

LUCKY: Well, at least she won't need to worry 'bout a limo. Look at this baby! Emily's gonna have the sweetest ride at prom.

CAMARO: You think I'm gonna let a bunch of seventeen-year-olds, with names like Blaise, drive this car?

ASTON: I already tried.

CAMARO: It's not like it'll start anyways

LUCKY: Ya know, Camaro, I was takin' a look at the engine—

CAMARO: —You were doin' what?

LUCKY: I think it might be a simple fix.

CAMARO: What the fuck were you doin' messin' // with the engine?

ASTON: Camaro, take it // easy.

LUCKY: I barely touched it. // I just kinda looked around.

CAMARO: Who gave you the fuckin' // right to do that!?

ASTON: Camaro!

LUCKY: I think you might just be missin' a piston ring.

CAMARO: No.

LUCKY: I mean, it happens to everyone. You're workin' on a project, day in, day out, everyday, ya start to overthink things and the answer is just starin' at ya in the face.

ASTON: Camaro, Lucky has a fresh set of eyes. Maybe she's right.

CAMARO: She's not.

ASTON: How can you be sure?

CAMARO: 'Cause I know that car and it ain't a piston ring.

LUCKY: Well, I bought one.

> *LUCKY takes a piston ring out of her pocket and places it on the table.*

From my guy at the junkyard.

ASTON: Camaro, let's give it try.

CAMARO: No.

ASTON: Today might be THE // day.

CAMARO: I said no. Drop it!

ASTON: What if she's right?

CAMARO: She's not right, okay. She's not. I know that fuckin' car. I know that fuckin' engine. I know what it is supposed to fuckin' sound like and I would notice if it was missin' a fuckin' piston ring. I wouldn't miss somethin' like that. I stare at that fuckin' engine all day so I would know if it was a fuckin' piston ring and it's not a fuckin' piston ring so drop it!

> *CAMARO picks up the piston ring and throws it in the trash.*

ASTON: Camaro!

LUCKY: I'm sorry, I didn't mean to // upset you.

ASTON: Don't apologize. Camaro should.

CAMARO: She promised me she wouldn't touch // the engine.

LUCKY: I barely touched it // I just wanted to help.

ASTON: You sound like a five-year-old, // Camaro.

CAMARO: I'm not Emily, // Aston.

LUCKY: Guys, it's okay, seriously it's fine. This is not how I wanted this to go. It was supposed to be a good thing... I dunno, a happy note to lighten the mood. Like, I dunno, if the car starts it was a good omen or some shit.

CAMARO: Good omen for what?

LUCKY: Camaro, Aston, sometimes the best families are the ones ya get to choose and I'm happy you all chose me. No matter where I go, IF I go, I'll always remember this place as home, 'cause of you.

CAMARO: You goin' somewhere?

ASTON: The waitlist...

LUCKY: I'm in. I got in.

ASTON: Oh my God...

CAMARO: Got in? Where?

LUCKY: UCLA.

CAMARO: College?

LUCKY: I applied— on a whim— and first I was waitlisted and now I'm in. I got into their mechanical engineering department.

ASTON: Congratulations! Camaro...?

CAMARO: So, what does this mean?

LUCKY: Well, I haven't made my decision. I have a lot to think 'bout. There's a lot of movin' parts. So I dunno. It's a, it's a maybe.

CAMARO: California...

LUCKY: No one in my family has ever gone to college, but when I saw Professor Hamlin // in front of that class—

CAMARO: Who?

LUCKY: She shined. Fuck, she sparkled. I mean, just like this car. It was rusted and dirty and no one would know what the fuck it was capable of, but now... maybe I can do it too?

CAMARO: What do you want from me?

LUCKY: When I was thinkin' of goin' to college the first time, I went to my dad for advice. He said, "If ya ain't sweatin', ya ain't workin'." So, I just fell back in formation. But he's not around anymore so... what do you think I should do?

Pause.

CAMARO: Who do you think I am? // Seriously, look at me. Who am I to you?

ASTON: Camaro, stop!

LUCKY: Camaro, I don't—

CAMARO: —I'm not your mom, okay? Do what ya want.

ASTON: CAMARO.

Beat.

CAMARO: Mrs. Wilson brought in her Oldsmobile for an oil change. But it's definitely her exhaust. Handle that for me?

LUCKY: Yeah, yeah... I got your six.

LUCKY exits to the second garage.

ASTON: I have never been that embarrassed in // my entire life.

CAMARO: How long did you know?

ASTON: Awhile.

CAMARO: We don't keep secrets from each other.

ASTON: But apparently we change locks every year.

CAMARO: I gave you the new key, didn't I?

ASTON: After you had nothing else to hide.

CAMARO: Why didn't you warn me?

ASTON: Warn you?

CAMARO: You were the one. You were the one who convinced me to give that girl a job, give her a key, let 'er work on the car—

ASTON: —You brought her in first, over your own niece // might I add.

CAMARO: Don't try to distract with Emily. You told me, you said, "I gotta feelin' 'bout her."

ASTON: I did... I do. I still do have a feeling 'bout Lucky. I think she is good for this garage. I think she is good for you. She helps you get your head out of that god forsaken car so you can move on. Look at this car! Look at it! It's beautiful. It looks just like when Daddy had it. All it needs is to rev and it'll be gone and you can finally move on.

CAMARO: It needs to remember its purpose. It needs to find a heartbeat.

ASTON goes over to the trashcan and pulls out the piston.

ASTON: Try it.

CAMARO: Aston...

ASTON: She has a fresh set of eyes. She saw something you didn't.

CAMARO: Aston, no—

ASTON: —Why not? If it doesn't work, then I'll admit I was wrong.

CAMARO: Aston, I won't say it again.

ASTON: There's only one reason for you not to try.

CAMARO: [...]

ASTON: Camaro... Camaro... put the piston ring in.

CAMARO: Do you really want me to, now?

ASTON: Camaro, I put my life on hold for you. Five years. It took me five years. I had to ask for my tuition back.

CAMARO: [...]

ASTON: Put the piston—

CAMARO: —Are you fuckin' deaf, Denise?

Silence.

ASTON drops the piston ring. She tries to find words, but for the first time, she is speechless. She exits.

Lights fade.

End of Scene 10.

SCENE 11

Lights up on the garage, earlier the next morning. The garage is empty, except for the Chevy. CAMARO enters from the swinging door dressed in her jumpsuit, carrying a beer. Her anger carries over from the previous scene. She finishes chugging her beer and aggressively throws it into a corner. Her shoulders slump and she braces herself on the Chevy's engine. It immediately calms her. Camaro smiles, pulls the piston ring out of her pocket, and secures it in the engine. She gets in the driver's side and starts the car. We hear the engine rev. Camaro slides over to the passenger seat and closes her eyes. We hear the sound of a car door opening and closing as Camaro imagines someone getting into the car. We hear the car pull out then, wind blowing through a window. Camaro is traveling down Route 66 with her father in the driver's seat. The faint tune of "My Girl" is mixed in with the ambiance of highway driving. Finally, all the sounds fade and we hear peaceful ocean waves. Camaro starts softly, sweetly singing the chorus of "My Girl."

CAMARO: "Well I guess you'd say

What can make me feel this way?

My girl (my girl, my girl)"

She opens her eyes and looks to the empty driver's seat.

LUCKY unlocks the outside door and enters.

LUCKY: Oh my God!

CAMARO immediately turns the engine off and jumps out of the car.

Oh my God! Oh my... fuck! It works! Camaro! It works! Ya got it to rev!

CAMARO: Shut up!

LUCKY: What's wrong with ya? This is awesome!

CAMARO: No, it's not.

LUCKY: Camaro, ya got it to rev.

CAMARO: No, I didn't.

LUCKY: I know an engine revvin' when I hear it.

CAMARO: Well, ya heard wrong. That's not what the engine is supposed to sound like.

LUCKY: What's it supposed to sound like?

CAMARO: Like a heart beatin'.

LUCKY: Is everythin' okay?

CAMARO: Why are you here?

LUCKY: 'Cause it's almost 8:00 a.m. and I work here.

CAMARO: Do you? 'Cause it sounds like your bags are already packed.

LUCKY: I got in, but I haven't made a // decision yet.

CAMARO: Oh bull fuckin' shit! If that were true, you never woulda applied in the first place.

LUCKY: I didn't think I'd get in. No one in my family // ever went—

CAMARO: —Goin' to California. What? Southside ain't good enough for you?

LUCKY: No... that's not—

CAMARO: —The Southside was good enough for your dad. He knew right where he belonged with all us greasy, dirty, filthy people. But I guess that's not good enough for you. You wanna get yourself all shined up and walk on that campus like you belong, but lemme tell you somethin', your hands will always be dirty. People are gonna see the grime under your nails and they ain't gonna wanna touch you.

LUCKY: I thought it wouldn't hurt to try.

CAMARO: No, it didn't hurt YOU.

Before you came around I was alone in the trenches. I just gave up hope of savin' this place. And then, PRAISE THE LORD! HALLELUJAH! My luck changed 'cause the honorable Sergeant Lucy Lucky Fuckin' Wells comes to the rescue. You said you had my six. You ain't nuthin' but a swerver. Left instead of a right. Some fuckin' Marine you turned out to be.

LUCKY: No. Don't.

CAMARO: Don't tell me what I can and I can't do in my goddamn garage. You ain't a sergeant in here.

LUCKY: Camaro, I am warning you—

CAMARO: —I wished I was warned 'bout you. You're nuthin' but a scared li'l girl that got too wrapped up in somethin' and now you wanna run away instead of takin' responsibility.

LUCKY: I know what I said, but it ain't just me in this garage. If it goes under... don't blame me for your mistakes.

CAMARO: Oh, so I'm not good enough for you. This garage, this life that you happily walked into ain't good enough for you? Fuck you.

LUCKY: You know what... I'm gonna go—

CAMARO: —What? And tell Aston what you think you heard today?

LUCKY: Whatever's goin' on between you and your sister // ain't my business.

CAMARO: Gonna go and whisper your li'l secrets to each other. Lie and say you heard it rev.

LUCKY: It wouldn't be a lie.

Pause.

CAMARO: You get this fuckin' straight. You ain't gonna say shit, hear me? You wouldn't understand. You didn't hear a car rev. This car ain't leavin' 'til I hear its heartbeat!

> *LUCKY prepares to leave. CAMARO grabs a tire iron.*

Get out! Go. I'm used to it. Everyone always leaves nuthin' but a BIG empty space behind.

> *CAMARO approaches LUCKY who is standing near the Chevy.*

Just a big ol' empty space, but this car ain't fuckin' goin' nowhere.

> *CAMARO swings the tire iron. She hits the Chevy. (She was <u>not</u> aiming for LUCKY). Camaro continues her destruction of the car. Lucky stands aside and watches in shock.*

Just want somethin' to fill the space! FILL IT! FILL IT! But you wanna leave! An empty space! Leave! Leave! Well, now it can't leave! It can't leave an empty space!

> *LUCKY tires to interfere, but CAMARO pushes her off.*

LEAVE! GO! This ain't your home no more!

> *LUCKY hesitates, but then backs out the door.*

> *Lights fade.*

> *End Scene 11.*

SCENE 12

Lights up on the garage. Still May, the following week. CAMARO sits in the Chevy Camaro. The destruction of the car is now complete. One door is ripped off and lays on the floor. The mirror dangles at the side of the car. A tire or two is flattened. The paint is scratched with dents to the body and the windshield is almost shattered.

Bell rings. A customer is waiting.

CAMARO *(shouting from the car)*: We're closed!

> *ASTON enters carrying a pie. She takes in the destruction.*

ASTON: I didn't wanna believe it.

CAMARO: [...]

ASTON: You've been closed for a week straight. That's not gonna make customers happy.

CAMARO: [...]

ASTON: So, do you just live here now?

CAMARO: [...]

ASTON: Aunt Rita called. She was concerned. I told her you were sick. She made you a pie. Here's your God damn pie.

> *She slams the pie on the table without a care.*

CAMARO: [...]

ASTON: I swear to God, Camaro, if you do not say something in the next 5 seconds I'm going to-

> *Beat.*

I hit her.

> *CAMARO immediately turns around.*

She's going to Moraine.

CAMARO: But what 'bout—

ASTON: —The deadline to let all of her schools know if she was attending was May 15th.

CAMARO: Yesterday.

ASTON: She told me today she wants to go to Moraine.

CAMARO: Maybe there's still time. // You can call someone.

ASTON: I hit her. One slap right across the face. This time... it wasn't crocodile tears. Those were real. I stared at her and you know what I saw? Me. Me when I was her age.

> *CAMARO jumps out of the car and wraps ASTON in an embrace.*

CAMARO: It's okay. It's okay…

ASTON: I didn't know where else to go. Steve wouldn't understand—

CAMARO: —You come here, ya hear me? You come be with your people. You're only human. Humans make horrible, fuckin' mistakes, but you'll learn from it. I know that you'll learn from it. She's gonna be fine. You'll see. She's going to be fine.

ASTON: What did you do?

CAMARO: I fucked up. I fucked up really big, Aston.

ASTON: I've seen you fix bigger wrecks in less than a month… and I'll help you fix it.

CAMARO: No! You've done enough.

ASTON: What's family for? And I got some money saved.

CAMARO *(choking on tears)*: I'm sorr—

> *ASTON wraps CAMARO in an embrace.*

ASTON: Don't apologize. You're horrible at it.

> *Beat.*

You gotta forgive her, Camaro.

CAMARO: Of course I will! If she comes back to the shop—

ASTON: —No… I mean your mom.

CAMARO: How the fuck can you even say that? She left us. Both of us. She dropped us off at school, swerved left instead of right, and we never saw her again.

ASTON: She's a human being too. But the good news is, you don't have to make amends for her. She made peace with her choice a long time ago. Stop looking to the past, instead, build on it.

> *Silence. CAMARO looks to the outside door.*

She'll come back.

CAMARO: How do you—

ASTON: —I gotta feeling.

> *Lights fade.*
>
> *End Scene 12.*

SCENE 13

*Lights up on the garage. A few days later from Scene 12.
CAMARO is on the phone. The debris around the car has
been cleaned up.*

CAMARO: Yes... yes Mrs. Wilson, I understand... but ya see, Mrs. Wilson it's not just an oil change... uh huh... but the crankin', the coughin', the car shakin' has nuthin' to do with the oil, your car is just old... I know... I know...

The bell rings. A customer is waiting.

Mrs. Wilson, I understand that ya had the car for a long time, it's familiar, ya feel safe in it, but sometimes things get old and there's nuthin' bringin' them back. Ya gotta let it go to make room for somethin' better.

LUCKY enters from the swinging door. CAMARO smiles. Lucky goes to her jumpsuit.

—Yes, I'm still here. The money ya'd get from the parts of your car would be a very nice down payment on a brand new car. And you and Mr. Wilson can go on nice road trips together and... Yeah, they absolutely make SUVs big enough to fit all your cats... okay... okay! I'll take a look and give ya an estimate. You have a good day, Mrs. Wilson.

CAMARO hangs up the phone.

Hi.

LUCKY: Got your call.

CAMARO: I'm not good at this.

LUCKY: Then let's just get to work.

CAMARO: Did you send the email? Did you tell them ya weren't comin'?

LUCKY: I wrote it. It's sittin' in my drafts. I gotta feelin', somethin' told me to wait. I wanted to be sure you'd lemme back.

CAMARO: Good, well, let 'em know you're on your way.

CAMARO tosses LUCKY the keys to the Chevy Camaro.

LUCKY: What is this?

CAMARO: Last I checked, the orange line doesn't go to California. And I don't wanna hear 'bout how expensive plane tickets are. There's more than enough room for you and some boxes in that car. The rest I will help ya ship.

LUCKY: Camaro, there is no way—

CAMARO: —Don't make excuses.

LUCKY: This is your dad's car. This is your dad.

CAMARO: This car is what brought him from California to Chicago. This car's whole purpose is to chase after somethin'. I'm not runnin' after anythin' and it deserves to go back home.

LUCKY: This, this is fucked, okay? College for me is... I made my decision, okay? I love it here! I mean, look at you. You worked here your whole life and you turned out great!

CAMARO: I don't want you to be like me. Look, I dunno if this is God, the universe, or just dumb fuckin' luck, but what I do know is you got a shot.

LUCKY: I'm not leavin' my home.

CAMARO: Do you know why we call Route 66 the beginnin' AND the end? 'Cause the sign says Route 66 STARTS at Adams and Michigan, but there is another sign on Jackson where Route 66 ends. You start at Adams and Michigan, south to Springfield, then St. Louis, cut through Oklahoma, Texas, New Mexico, Arizona, and in ten days, California. But then, you can turn around. You can always come home.

LUCKY: What should the rev sound like?

CAMARO: Like a heartbeat.

> *CAMARO goes to fridge and grabs two Old Styles. LUCKY goes around to the passenger side of the car and holds the door open for Camaro. Camaro gets in, reaches over, and unlocks the driver's side door. Lucky gets in and grips the steering wheel.*

LUCKY: For Mr. Gibson.

LUCKY & CAMARO: Old Style sittin' in the console

Wind blowin' through the window

When the rubber meets the concrete

Ya get down on your knees

Pray for your shot

Grab life by the balls and give it all ya got.

> *They spit.*

LUCKY: To the beginnin' of the end.

CAMARO: The end AND the beginnin'.

> *LUCKY turns the key. The engine coughs, sputters, and dies.*
>
> *Pause.*

Daddy was always a stubborn man. Do it again.

> *LUCKY starts the car again. The engine revs, only this time, it sounds like a heartbeat.*
>
> *Lights fade.*
>
> *End of Scene 13.*

SCENE 14

*Lights up on the garage. It's June. The Chevy Camaro is no
longer there. CAMARO is using a push broom to sweep up
any debris. ASTON enters this time from the audience. The
garage door is open. She carries with her a Dunkin' Donuts
bag, one hot coffee, and one iced coffee.*

ASTON: How in this God-made world can you drink hot coffee in June?

CAMARO: I like what I like.

> *ASTON hands CAMARO the coffee and strawberry glazed
> donut.*

ASTON: I was sweating just holding that.

CAMARO: I love Chicago in June. Threat of snow is officially gone and ya can
finally work with the garage open.

> *They stand admiring the fresh breeze filling the big, empty
> space.*

ASTON: She left?

CAMARO: Yesterday mornin'. Summer classes start in 'bout two weeks. She
wanted to take her time and enjoy the drive.

ASTON: Where is she?

CAMARO: Last she called, she made it to St. Louis. She'll be cuttin' through
the Ozarks tomorrow.

> *Beat.*

ASTON: I brought you a surprise?

CAMARO: Veggie egg white?

ASTON: I learned my lesson. Here… Emily's prom photos finally came in.

CAMARO: I get to finally see?

ASTON: I wanted you to see them professionally done.

> *ASTON hands CAMARO a folder with the photos. Camaro flips
> through them.*

CAMARO: Did the Vegas showgirl find her Cinderella—

> *She sees a photo of the dress.*

Holy shit! Is that my niece?! My curly Sue?

ASTON: Gorgeous isn't she.

CAMARO: That dress.

ASTON: Yeah…!

CAMARO: Fuck! I'm even jealous! That thing is…

ASTON: Perfect. A dream.

CAMARO: Aston... I can tell from the photo that had to cost some cash.

ASTON: Rude.

CAMARO: Aston...

ASTON: ...five hundred dollars.

CAMARO: ASTON GIBSON! Are you crazy?

ASTON: It's alright.

CAMARO: Alright?! Five hundred dollars for a prom dress!

ASTON: —What? She looks beautiful, perfect, happy... Besides, I had the money saved.

CAMARO: You didn't! Aston! That was for you to be // happy.

ASTON: I still got the ten dollars left. Now, before you gimme that look like, "I just bought her the dress out of guilt—"

CAMARO: —Aston...

ASTON: I am not some fragile, wilting flower of a mother! I was raised by the same daddy you were.

CAMARO: Five hundred dollars though...

ASTON: After I left the shop and went home that day, I expected Emily to have locked herself in her room, just like I used to do. But you wanna know something? I found her sitting on my bed: calm, cool, collected. She turned to me and said, "Mom, we need to talk."

CAMARO: Shit...

ASTON: Right! So, I sit down and she proceeds to tell me how she broke up with Blaise.

CAMARO: Why am I just hearin' 'bout this now!?

ASTON: 'Cause I wanted to hand you those photos and say, "Blaise is out of the picture."

CAMARO: How?

ASTON: Recently, she's been getting tired of Blaise's immaturity and Bebe being, quote, "so fake that for someone who touts a picture perfect suburban family, might be having an affair with some Mercedes Benz car dealer."

CAMARO (sigh/eye roll): New Lenox...

ASTON: Right. So one day, she finds a photo of her perfect prom dress.

CAMARO: The one she's wearin'.

ASTON: And the model looked just like her. Gorgeous, glowing, with a head full of curls. She got so excited, she showed it to Blaise and all Blaise could say was, "But, you're not gonna wear your hair like that, right?" Lemme tell you something, Camaro, there is no doubt she is my daughter after what she said to that boy.

CAMARO: Why Moraine?

ASTON: Emily told me the reason she wants to go to community college is NOT 'cause of Blaise, but 'cause she doesn't know what she wants to do. She realized how much money I spent on her tuition to go to some private school with a drama program she didn't even use. So, instead of spending all that money on a four-year college, she'll go to Moraine for two years, get her gen ed's out of the way, and figure out what she wants to do.

CAMARO: Wow... my niece.

ASTON: My daughter.

CAMARO: She's just like you.

ASTON: I felt refreshed. Like I was looking at a completely new person. Someone I had never met before living in my own house. And then bam... // I gotta feeling.

CAMARO: You gotta feelin'.

ASTON: I grabbed my keys and Emily and we pulled into that boutique and there it was.

It fit perfectly, like it was waiting for her.

CAMARO: Amen.

ASTON: I could not buy the dress of my dreams. But I could for Emily.

CAMARO: I wouldn't of asked for any help if I knew—

ASTON: —You heard the heartbeat. Besides, I still got ten bucks left. What was I gonna do trotting around my hospital wing carrying pee samples in some Louboutins. I'll save it for when I get my own practice.

CAMARO: I got ya somethin' too.

ASTON: Seeing the garage with a big, open space is enough.

> *CAMARO hands ASTON a folded piece of paper. ASTON skims the letter.*

CAMARO: You just gotta sign the bottom and it's official.

ASTON: "Gibson Daughters' Automotive Repair Shop..."?

CAMARO: It's always been your home. But now ya got papers too.

ASTON: You changed the name?

CAMARO: Yeah, I'm the boss, I can do that. In fact, here help me out.

> *CAMARO goes over to the old "Gibson & Sons" sign and takes it down.*

Hand me that block on the table.

> *ASTON picks up the wooden block and hands it to CAMARO who hangs it in place. The sign reads, "Gibson Daughters."*

How's it look?

ASTON: Camaro—

CAMARO: —Don't. You got work to do now.

ASTON: Like what?

CAMARO: Ya gotta help me hire people.

ASTON: You want me to help you hire people? From where?

CAMARO: Whoever applies. This place is huge now. It'll speed up business for sure, now that we got a garage free.

ASTON: Hire outside the family...?

CAMARO: I know change can be hard.

ASTON: I think we should take some baby steps. Emily still needs a summer job—

CAMARO: —Hard. No.

> *The bell rings. A customer is waiting.*

And it begins...

ASTON: She coming home?

CAMARO: Said she'd make it home for Second Christmas.

ASTON: Good. Lemme know when she calls again. Tell her I'm praying she makes it safely.

CAMARO: She's with Daddy. He knows the way.

> *ASTON exits. Lights start to fade on CAMARO sweeping. She begins humming the tune to "My Girl."*
>
> *Blackout.*

END OF PLAY

SET DRESSINGS

- Random tools
- Car parts
- Pumps
- Mini fridge
  - Old Style beer
- Coat rack with an extra jumpsuit hanging on it
- Wood carved sign in the middle of garage that says "Gibson & Sons"
- Metal work table
- Chest-high counter with a landline phone
- Trashcan

CHARACTER PROPS

- A brown bag from Dunkin' Donuts and coffee
  - Veggie egg white flatbread sandwich
  - Strawberry glazed donuts
  - Chocolate Long Johns
- Vintage 1967 Chevy Camaro steering wheel
- Sets of keys for:
  - The Chevy Camaro
  - The office door (one for Camaro, one for Aston)
  - The garage door
  - Aston's car
- Resumé
- 2 Chevy Camaro piston rings
- 2 Chevy Camaro doors
- 4 tires for the Chevy Camaro
- Speed drill
- Tire iron
- Aston's large purse
  - Thermal socks
  - Large binder with bow on top
  - Forever 21 gift card
  - Checkbook with checks
  - Pen
  - Notice of final payment letter
- 2 small wrapped packages (one with fudge, the other with a set of keys)
- Car paint gun
- Pie
- Iced coffee
- Deed to the Automotive Repair Shop
- Envelope with prom photos
- Wood carved sign that says "Gibson Daughters"
- Push broom
- Wad of cash

ABOUT STAGE RIGHTS

Based in Los Angeles and founded in 2000, Stage Rights is one of the foremost independent theatrical publishers in the United States, providing stage performance rights for a wide range of plays and musicals to theater companies, schools, and other producing organizations across the country and internationally. As a licensing agent, Stage Rights is committed to providing each producer the tools they need for financial and artistic success. Stage Rights is dedicated to the future of live theatre, offering special programs that champion new theatrical works.

To view all of our current plays and musicals, visit:

www.stagerights.com

CPSIA information can be obtained
at www.ICGtesting.com
Printed in the USA
LVHW111611040822
725208LV00004B/514

9 780692 798515